A New Analysis of Urbanization in China

Chu Tianjiao
Wang Guoping
Zhu Yuan

Published by
ACA Publishing Ltd.
University House
11-13 Lower Grosvenor Place,
London SW1W 0EX, UK
Tel: +44 (0)20 7834 7676 Fax: +44 (0)20 7973 0076
E-mail: info@alaincharlesasia.com

Web:www.alaincharlesasia.com
Beijing Office
Tel:+86(0)10 8472 1250 Fax:86(0)10 5885 0639
Written by Liu Jingbei
Edited by David Lammie, ACA Publishing Ltd
Translated by Liu Quanfu
© People's Publishing House, 2015
This translation is published by ACA Publishing Ltd in association with People's Publishing House

ALL RIGHTS RESERVED. NO PART OF THIS
PUBLICATION MAY BE REPRODUCED IN MATERIAL FORM,
BY ANY MEANS, WHETHER GRAPHIC,
ELECTRONIC, MECHANICAL OR OTHER, INCLUDING
PHOTOCOPYING OR INFORMATION STORAGE, IN
WHOLE OR IN PART, AND MAY NOT BE USED TO PREPARE
OTHER PUBLICATIONS WITHOUT WRITTEN
PERMISSION FROM THE PUBLISHER.

The greatest care has been taken to ensure accuracy but the publisher can accept no responsibility for errors or omissions, or for any liability occasioned by relying on its content.
ISBN 978-1-910760-08-6
A New Analysis of Urbanization in China is available from the National Bibliographic Service of the British Library.

Preface

What is the state system of China? How has the Communist Party of China (CPC) managed to exercize long-term governance and to lead the Chinese people from one victory to another? What are the 'secrets' of the CPC's governance? What is China's development road? What significant strategies have been adopted in China? What is the next step in China's development? Why has China been able to achieve such rapid economic development? These are just some of the many questions frequently asked by the international community, especially foreign political parties and statesmen on their visits to China. For the purpose of providing answers to these questions and enabling readers to be informed about the real China and the CPC, we arranged for the *Understanding Modern China* Series (hereinafter referred to as the Series) to be written, to serve as elementary documents introducing the CPC, as well as China's development road, development theories and development experience.

The Series is inspired by the new philosophies, new ideas and new strategies for the country's governance put forward by General Secretary Xi Jinping since the 18th National Congress of the CPC, aimed at the following aspects: strenuously reflecting the development vision of 'the Chinese Dream' and the development prospects of the 'Two Centenary' goals; strenuously reflecting the coordinated promotion of the overall situation of a 'five-pronged approach to building socialism with Chinese characteristics to build up socialist economy, socialist democracy, socialist advanced culture, socialist harmonious society and socialist ecological civilisation; and the strategic arrangements for the 'Four-Pronged Comprehensive Strategy' comprehensively completing the building of a moderately prosperous society in all respects, comprehensively deepening reform in all respects, comprehensively advancing the rule of law, and comprehensively exercising strict discipline for the party; strenuously reflecting the 'new normal' facilitating and leading China's economic development and the implementation of the 'five major development concepts' to promote innovative, coordinated, green, open and shared development; strenuously reflecting the three major economic development strategies of the 'Belt and Road', the coordinated development of Beijing, Tianjin and Hebei province, and the Yangtze river economic belt. On the basis of a great number of fresh cases and experiences, the Series tells China's story, transmits China's voice, analyzes China's problems, and offers China solutions.

The Series has been written on the basis of telling China's story and transmitting China's voice, oriented around the following four aspects: the first is to illustrate the new measures taken to deepen reform since the 18th National Congress of the CPC, the new ideas on economic development and the new philosophy on foreign affairs, on the basis of an all-round introduction to the achievements since the reform and opening up; the second is to analyze the reason for the achievements, the underlying operating law, and the process of evolution, while presenting the development achievements of China's economy and society; the third is to keep to problem orientation and demand orientation, rather than attempt to be all-embracing and systematic, so as to clear up targeted doubts and confusion on the basis of the demands of foreign readers; the fourth is to introduce China not only in terms of 'where it is coming from', but also in terms of 'where it is going', for the purpose of enabling readers to know about China's historical development process on the one hand, and on the other hand, exemplifying and clarifying how China assures the organic unification of its past, present and future, the organic combination of legacy and innovation, and how China is planning its future development.

Under the guidance of the International Department of the CPC Central Committee, the writing of the Series has been organized by China Executive Leadership Academy Pudong (CELAP).

The International Department of the CPC Central Committee is the functional department of the CPC in charge of foreign affairs. So far, the CPC has established connections of various types with more than 600 political parties and organizations in over 160 countries and regions, which include left-wing and right-wing parties; both ruling parties and opposition parties. Foreign affairs work is of paramount importance to the CPC, and an indispensable component of national diplomacy as a whole, whose target is to promote state-to-state and people-to-people communication and understanding.

Preface

CELAP is a national leadership institution in China, and as a platform on which international cooperative training and exchange are carried out, CELAP has held fast to its characteristics of internationality and openness since March 2005 when it was founded. CELAP spares no effort in implementing international cooperative training, with target participants being foreign political parties and statesmen, high-ranking business executives and senior professionals. By the end of 2015, CELAP had offered training programs to more than 6,000 participants from over 130 countries, and thus has won wide recognition and received a favorable reception from the countries, regions and participants that are involved.

To cater for the needs of foreign participants, CELAP initiated the writing of the Series at the beginning of 2012, and after four years of modifications and improvements, the finalized manuscripts were completed at the end of 2015. The first batch of 10 books to be published in this Series are: *China's New Strategies for Governing the Country*; *The Communist Party of China: the Past, Present and Future of Party Building*; *China's Reform, Opening Up and Construction of Development Zones*; *The Framework of the Chinese Government and Public Services*; *A New Analysis of Urbanization in China*; *China's Agriculture and Rural Development in the Post-Reform Era*; *The Evolution of China's Diplomacy in the Modern Era*; *Leadership Selection and Appointment in China*; *Leadership Education and Training in China*; and *Shanghai – the 'Pacesetter' of China's Reform and Opening Up*.

The authors of the Series are mainly professionals in CELAP, and functionaries and specialists in the Development Research Center of the Shanghai Municipal People's Government, Shanghai Institute for International Studies and Hangzhou Research Center for Urban Studies.

The Series is published in Chinese and English, with the English translation done mainly by senior professors at Shanghai International Studies University, to whom thanks are due. Gratitude also goes to the People's Publishing House for its great support and positive suggestions in the process of writing and translating.

Writing such a series of textbooks for mature foreign students is a first in China. Constructive criticism is welcome, for the Series as a new endeavor can hardly be free from mistakes.

Editorial Committee of the *Understanding Modern China* Series
January 2016

The Editorial Committee of the Understanding Modern China Series

Directors: Guo Yezhou Feng Jun

Vice Directors: Zhou Zhongfei   An Yuejun

Members: (Listed alphabetically)

An Yuejun	Chen Zhong	Feng Jun
Guo Yezhou	He Lisheng	Jiang Haishan
Li Man	Li Yanhui	Liu Genfa
Liu Jingbei	Wang Guoping	Wang Jinding
Yang Jiemian	Zhao Shiming	Zheng Jinzhou
Zhou Zhenhua	Zhou Zhongfei	

Editor-in-Chief: Feng Jun

Alain Charles Asia (ACA) Publishing Ltd is delighted to be associated with the People's Publishing House to bring this series of 10 *Understanding Modern China* books to an English-speaking readership.

ACA, formerly known as ACP (Alain Charles Publishing) Ltd Beijing, was founded in October 1989 and was the first foreign-owned publishing company to be allowed to open an office in China.

In 2007, ACP Beijing was renamed ACA Publishing Ltd to better reflect its focus on China and the Asia-Pacific region. The company specialises in publishing books about China for international readers and has offices in Beijing and London.

ACA Publishing Ltd,

April 2016

Contents

Introduction X

1. Ongoing Urbanization in China 1
    I. Development and Current Situation 1
    II. Challenges and Problems 9
    III. New Urbanization Strategies and Solutions 16

2. Development of Urban-rural Planning in China 24
    I. Urban-rural Planning in China since 1949 24
    II. Designers and Executives of Urban-rural Planning in China ..33
    III. Drafting, Modification and Implementation of Urban-rural Planning 39

3. Industrial Distribution in Cities 46
    I. Dominant Functions of Cities and Their Industrial Layout 46
    II. Construction of Development Zones: a New Industrial Space ..52
    III. Development of New Urban Districts: Reconstruction of Industrial Space 61

4. Construction of Urban Infrastructure in China 68
    I. History of the Construction of Urban Infrastructure in China ..68
    II. Problems with the Construction of Urban Infrastructure in China 73
    III. Exploration into the Construction of Urban Infrastructure in China 76

5. Management of Urban Land in China 83
    I. Property Rights of Urban Land 83
    II. Utilization and Management of Urban Land 87
    III. Management of the Urban Land Market 95

6. Management of Urban Communities 103

    I. Evolution of the Urban Community Management System 103

    II. Urban Community Services in China 112

    III. Self-governance of Urban Communities 120

7. Protection of Urban Historical and Cultural Heritage in China 125

    I. Protection of Urban Historical and Cultural Heritage in China: Past and Present 125

    II. Protection of Urban Cultural Relics and Historical Sites in China 128

    III. Protection of Historical and Cultural Street Districts in Chinese Cities 132

    IV. Protection of Historical Cities in China 138

Chapter Follow-up Questions and References 144

Introduction

Urbanization, an inexorable trend of economic and social development, can act as a benchmark to gauge the economic and societal progress of a country or region. Over the past six decades or so since the founding of the People's Republic of China (PRC), and especially since the reform and opening-up process was launched, we have witnessed a marked upward spike in China's urbanization. With a population of 1.3 billion, China's urbanization will have a major impact on the development of the world as well as on the country itself. Joseph Eugene Stiglitz, the acclaimed American economist, notes that there will be two major events affecting the development of human society in the 21st century: one is the next round of the US-led new technological revolution, and the other is China's urbanization. The treasured efforts and practices of China, therefore, will make a significant contribution to global urbanization in the years to come.

1. Objectives

With time and space respectively as the vertical and horizontal axes, the authors of this book study urbanization in China to dynamically explore the evolution of the economy, society, ecology and culture associated with urbanization, to display the overall distinctive properties of urbanization in present-day China and to reveal the idea, the way and the experience of the country that is already well on its way to being urbanized. The ultimate objective is to acquaint readers with China's development strategy and philosophical outlook adopted in urbanization so that they may, in the long run, apply what they learn to their own local administration.

2. Framework

This book consists of seven chapters in total. Chapter One describes the past and the present of urbanization in China and comes up with some policies and measures for addressing current problems so as to ensure the sound development of China's urbanization.

The second chapter looks at the history of China's urban-rural planning since its inception, sums up the lessons and experience in its historical development, and then outlines the executive and operative systems, so that readers will have a global perspective of China's urban-rural planning.

Chapter Three reviews the evolution of the industrial layout and distribution in cities in China during its transition from a planned economy to a socialist market economy. It includes a detailed introduction to the establishment of development zones and construction of new towns or newly developed urban districts that function as the primary spatial carriers for the development of urban industries in China.

Chapter Four is devoted to elaborating on the impressive achievements, serviceable practices, overarching problems and workable countermeasures in China's urban infrastructure construction.

Chapter Five depicts the basic framework worked out since the implementation of reform and opening up for the paid use of urban land, with the focus on a detailed presentation of the property system, the management of utilization and the market regulation of urban land in China that gives an overall insight into China's urban land system.

Chapter Six reconsiders the evolution of the urban community management system in China, examines its background and the striking features that distinguish the system, and introduces the subject of urban community services and the self-management of urban communities in China.

By means of case analysis, the last chapter sums up China's practices in its effort to work out a graded or assorted protection of its historical and cultural heritage.

3. Highlights and Challenges

This book has a number of distinguishing features: by looking back to the recorded history of urbanization in China, the authors have dwelt on the perceived changes taking place in towns and cities since the start of reform and opening up and in the meantime expounded how the Chinese government has been working to set up and bring into force an institutional framework to guarantee that urbanization develops in a sustained way, so that readers will be well versed in China's realities and relevant background information that will help them further explore the development of urbanization in China.

The most challenging task for the authors is to address foreign readers' demands and interests, analyze the general features and requirements of cross-cultural communication, describe the national realities in plain but vivid language, narrate the history of China's urbanization by means of lively examples, and provide overseas students with teaching materials that are enjoyable, readable and pragmatic.

4. Directions

This book combines flexibility and openness in terms of its table of contents and teaching requirements as well as in the presentation and arrangement of chapters. Instructors, therefore, are encouraged to adopt an open and flexible teaching principle so that they can make the best use of it. The book is expected to have lasting relevance since the content of each chapter reflects the most basic and fundamental structure of knowledge; a coursebook compiled with a passive mentality would not be able to capture the latest state of affairs in China's urbanization. This being the case, all teachers are advised to energetically seek fresh information, keep on learning and acquire new skills so that they can stimulate interest in class. As for students, they should work to integrate or incorporate what they learn from this book with social realities so that they will have a deeper insight into the social and economic development in China.

Occasional slips are inevitable in a book and all suggestions will be highly appreciated. This book has been a joint effort: chapters one, two, three and five were written by Chu Tianjiao, while chapter four was jointly written by Chu Tianjiao and Zhu Yuan; chapter six was composed by Chen Zheng, while the concluding chapter was a joint effort between Li Mingchao and Shao Ying.

Chapter 1

Ongoing Urbanization in China

I. Development and Current Situation

Urbanization means a shift or transition of people who were dependent on agriculture to non-agricultural sectors, along with a growing intensification of production and pattern of life.[1] Urbanization in China, which accounts for a quarter of the population of all developing countries, will make a significant contribution to global urbanization in the 21st century. From 1975 to 2000, the urban population of the world increased by 1.317 billion, with an average annual growth of 52.68 million; out of this total, 1.164 billion were from developing countries, giving an average annual increase of 46.52 million. From 1978 to 2003, China's urban population increased by only 352 million, with an average annual growth of 14.05 million. This gave a growth rate that was just a quarter of the world average and approximately one third of that of developing countries during the same period. In years to come, the robust development of urbanization in China will help address many important issues and it will be regarded as one of the most positive aspects of human development in the 21st century.

1. Development and Current State

(1) Development phases of urbanization in China

Since the founding of the PRC in 1949, urbanization in the country can be broken down into two periods consisting of separate phases.

During the early years of the PRC, China adopted a strategy in which heavy industry was given top priority. Naturally, the implementation of the strategy made it necessary and even compulsory for many rural labor forces

---

[1] Zhou Ganzhi. *A Probe into Urbanization with Chinese Characteristics* [J]. *Urban Planning International*. 2009 (S1)

to move to state-owned enterprises (SOEs). This being the case, industrial cities, particularly those in inland China, were the first to enjoy preferential development. Consequently, the growth rate of China's urban population rapidly outstripped the growth rate of its total population. From 1952-1965, the urban population increased from 71.63 million to 130.45 million, with a growth rate of 82.1%. During this period, the overall population grew from 574.82 million to 725.38 million, with a growth rate of 26.2%. The percentage of the urban population increased to 18% in 1965, up from 12.5% in 1952 and 16.3% in 1958.

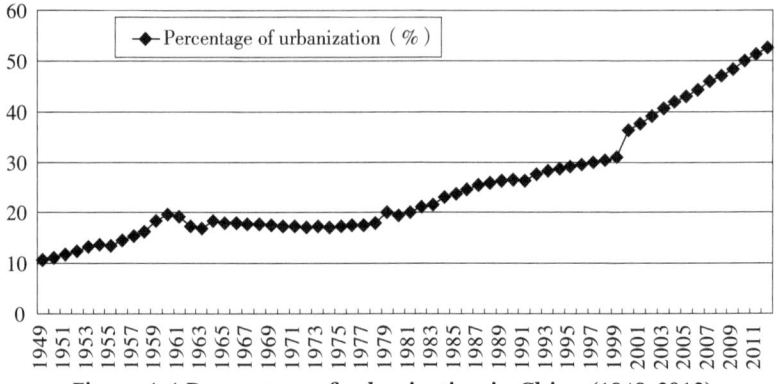

Figure 1-1 Percentage of urbanization in China (1949-2012)

A. Period of planned economy

i). 1952-1965: heavy industry prevails

During the early years of the PRC, China adopted a strategy in which heavy industry was given top priority. Naturally, the implementation of the strategy made it necessary and even compulsory for many rural labor forces to move to state-owned enterprises (SOEs). This being the case, industrial cities, particularly those in inland China, were the first to enjoy preferential development. Consequently, the growth rate of China's urban population rapidly outstripped the growth rate of its total population. From 1952-1965, the urban population increased from 71.63 million to 130.45 million, with a growth rate of 82.1%. During this period, the overall population grew from 574.82 million to 725.38 million, with a growth rate of 26.2%. The percentage of the urban population increased to 18% in 1965, up from 12.5% in 1952 and 16.3% in 1958.

When the First Five-year Plan was launched in 1953, China began to deploy a sizeable number of farmers for large-scale industrial construction. Industrialization spurred on urbanization and the urban population started to grow in a planned manner. The level of urbanization increased markedly to 16.25% in 1958 from 10.60% in 1949, with an annual growth rate of 0.63%. Under the system of the planned economy, those living in rural areas began to migrate steadily to cities via a recruitment drive, the urbanization rate standing at 15.4% in 1957 when the urban population multiplied to 100 million.

From 1958-1965, the number of residents living in urban areas changed radically. Between 1958 and the first half of 1960, the Chinese government, in an attempt to tap into its huge workforce, embarked on a massive investment drive and launched a campaign of socialist construction that sparked the 'Great Leap Forward' in industry and agriculture. In its empty pursuit of illusory economic advancement, the government embarked on the large-scale recruitment of workers in rural areas, which resulted in 30 million farmers moving into towns and cities. Those years represented the fastest growth in urbanization in the history of China, when the urbanization rate climbed by 1.45% annually. From 1963 to 1965, when food supplies failed to keep up with demand in cities because of a nationwide reduction in grain yield, 26 million people who had just entered cities had to be relocated to the countryside; during these two years, China experienced its most rapid decline in urbanization, when the annual rate fell to 1.0%.

ii). 1966-1978: the 'Cultural Revolution' is launched

The Cultural Revolution started in 1966, and the turmoil it inflicted did not come to an end until 1977. During these chaotic years, urbanization in China got bogged down and even regressed. On the one hand, the government appealed to more than 10 million urban youths to settle down in rural areas so as to alleviate unemployment and in the meantime the urban population fell by another 5 million when a huge number of government officials and intellectuals were mobilized to transfer to the countryside; on the other hand, the government injected a large amount of capital into the industrialization of inland areas where a great many military and heavy industrial enterprises that were formerly situated along coastal areas were relocated. Industrial construction went into operation on the basis of 'large distribution with small concentration', while plants and factories were built in locations that had to be 'close to mountains, scattered and sheltered'. Investment in urban construction was negligible at the time and, for that reason, there were few newly-built cities. From 1965-1975, the growth rate of China's overall population was higher than that of urban residents, with the percentage of the urban population being generally constant and staying much the same or even shrinking: 18% in 1965, 17.4% in 1970, 17.3% in 1975 and 17.9% in 1978.

B. Period of market economy

i). 1978-1996: urbanization rises after the start of reform and opening up

Beginning in 1978, China embarked on reform and opening up along with the adoption of a socialist market economy, and at the same time enacted policies that encouraged and promoted urbanization. Many counties were upgraded to cities and their number increased from 191 in 1978 to 666 in 1996. Meanwhile, the proportion of the urban population increased from 17.9% to 29.4%, China's urbanization level having soared by 11.8% in 18 years.

ii). After 1996: urbanization gathers pace with the deepening of reform and opening up

After 1996, urbanization in China started to develop at an ever quickening speed. The implementation of reform and opening up over the previous two decades facilitated economic progress, financial accumulation and income growth. It also promoted China's urbanization as a result of an upsurge in the construction of development zones, new urban districts and international metropolises. During the two decades, market demand for urbanization grew stronger than ever before when economic globalization helped open the economy wider to the outside world as the country sped up its marketization by means of economic restructuring. In the meantime, institutional innovation carried out by the government not only reduced transaction costs for urbanization, but also helped boost the expected rate of return with marked reduction of risks. These government and market factors made it possible for China's urbanization to enter a period of accelerating development, so much so that the urbanization rate snowballed from 29.4% in 1996 to 52.6% in 2012, the total urban population having increased from 359 million to 710 million.

2. Current Features

(1) Urbanization rate increasing at top speed for over three decades, a rare global phenomenon

Since the reform and opening up was implemented in 1978, the pace of urbanization in China has quickened, with small towns and cities emerging in large numbers. During this period, urbanization has expanded at around twice the world average speed. The progress of urbanization has varied among individual countries across the globe (see Figure 1-2); for example, the growth in urbanization level from 20% to 40% took 120 years to achieve in the UK, one century in France, eight decades in Germany, four decades in the US, three decades in the former Soviet Union and Japan, and 22 years in China. Even so, the urbanization level in China is still lower than the world average as well as the average in similarly industrialized countries.

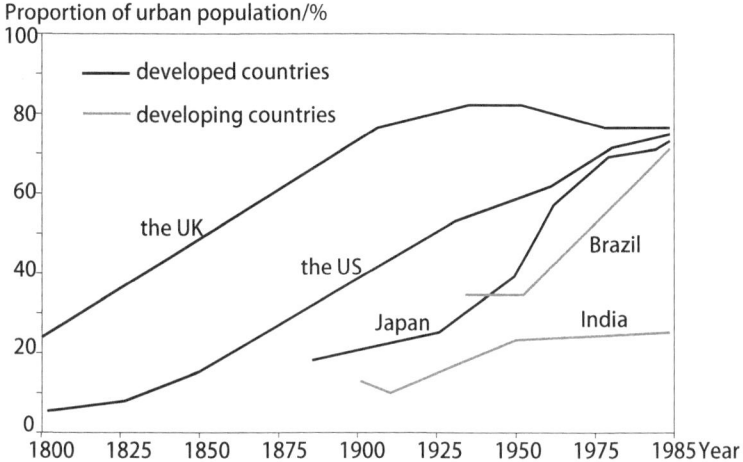

Figure 1-2 Evolution of urbanization rate in some countries

(2) Proliferation in urban residents primarily resulted from migration of rural people to urban areas, aside from natural growth; migrants and settled population to coexist for a long period

As China's household registration system became more flexible after reform and opening up, plenty of rural people moved into cities and better developed coastal areas. Large in number, extensive in range and far-reaching in influence, this labor force constituted the largest floating population ever seen in China's history. Floating peasant-workers started to become apparent in 1984. By the end of the 1980s, there were only 30 million migrant peasant-laborers, but after a number of ups and downs, the total reached 226 million by 2012. Since it was relatively difficult to move to urban areas, and particularly large cities, and because peasant-workers still had their own land and property back in their home towns and villages, of those who left home for cities, only 17% settled down to become urban residents; the remaining 83% were like migratory birds. This phenomenon contrasts with what happened in some European countries, where urbanization was initially the result of bankrupt farmers. Though a floating population can benefit both the migrants' old and new destinations, it is definitely a hindrance to the growth of industrial technology and upgrading of urbanization. It is only natural that some peasant-workers will not be accepted as permanent urban residents, and so the floating population will not evaporate in the immediate future.

(3) China's urbanization is burgeoning, driven by both secondary and tertiary industries, of which the latter will ultimately prevail

China's urbanization is now at an intermediate stage. As is shown in the history of world urbanization, a country will enter the stage of rapid development when the rate of urbanization reaches 30%; its progress will slow down when the rate stands at 70%. In 1978, the percentage of China's urban population was 17.92%. By 1996, however, the rate rose to as high as 30.48%. We may well say that China's urbanization gathered pace from then on and the share of the urban population climbed to 43.9% by 2006.[2] That is to say, the proportion of urban residents rose during the decade at an annual growth of 1.34%, which was nearly twice the rate recorded between 1978 and 1996 when the annual increase was only 0.7%. By the end of 2012, the proportion of the urban population rose to 52.6% and China's urbanization was growing at an annual rate of 1.54% during the five years from 2007 to 2012. In this light, urbanization in China is now developing at an accelerating speed, the essential feature of it being the quick but steady expansion of the urban population (see Figure 1-3).

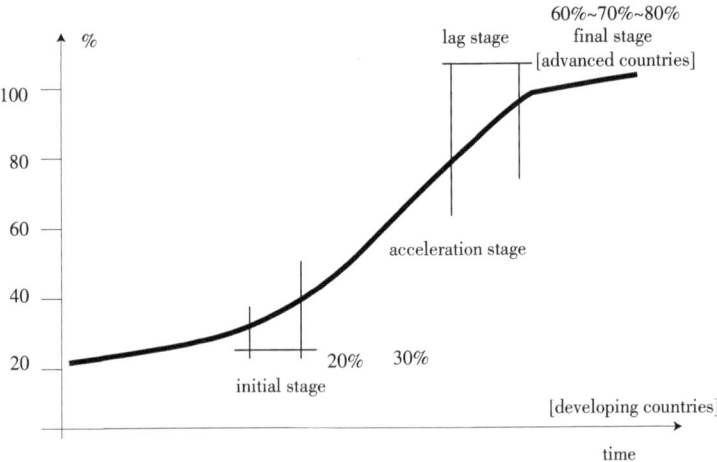

Figure 1-3 Developmental stages of urbanization

Primary industry has been a mainstay of China's overall industrial development and a major source of urban employment, though the tertiary industry will feature more prominently in the process of

---

[2] See *China Statistical Yearbook* (2007), page 105

urbanization in years to come. In 2012, the share of primary, secondary and tertiary industries was respectively 10.1%, 45.3% and 44.6% in China's industrial structure. According to the *Development Report on China's Floating Population* (2013), data collected by the National Health and Family Planning Commission of the PRC in 2013 showed that the proportion of manufacturing employees among China's floating population was 33.3%, which was 4.1% lower than that in 2011. In the same year, however, employee numbers in the tertiary sector multiplied, with the percentages of those employed in wholesale and retail and catering industries being 20.1% and 11.3% respectively, which were 2% and 1.4% higher than those in 2011. This being the case, secondary and tertiary industries born out of urbanization will become the primary driving forces in China's urbanization in years to come.

(4) Twin effect of government dominance and market forces in urbanization

China began to exercise the policy of reform and opening up in 1978. On the one hand, the government offered to facilitate the country's urbanization, believing that this was one of the central solutions to issues pertaining to agriculture, rural development and farmers. In its 10th Five-year Plan, the government advanced the strategy that urbanization must be accelerated and that some of the policies previously stipulated to deter rural residents from entering cities must be revised. In the 11th Five-year Plan, the government further proposed that urbanization must proceed in a sound way. On the other hand, urbanization clearly gathered pace after the market mechanism was applied to the relocation and employment of the labor force, the development of real estate and construction of urban infrastructure. At a work conference on urbanization held by the CPC Central Committee in December 2013, the government made it clear that urbanization must be people-centered so as to improve the caliber of urban residents and the quality of their lives; and besides, the regular 'citizenization' of the resident population who have the capacity to be employed and earn a decent living in cities must be given top priority. It further underscored the fact that urbanization entailed both the decisive role of the market in resource allocation and the indispensable functions of government in creating an institutional environment, working out development plans, constructing infrastructure, providing public services and reinforcing social governance. In the final analysis, the Party Central Committee was responsible for the stipulation of fundamental policies and determination of the overall planning and strategic layout of urbanization, while local governments should be realistic in carrying out general planning, working out relevant programs and handling operation and management in a creative way.

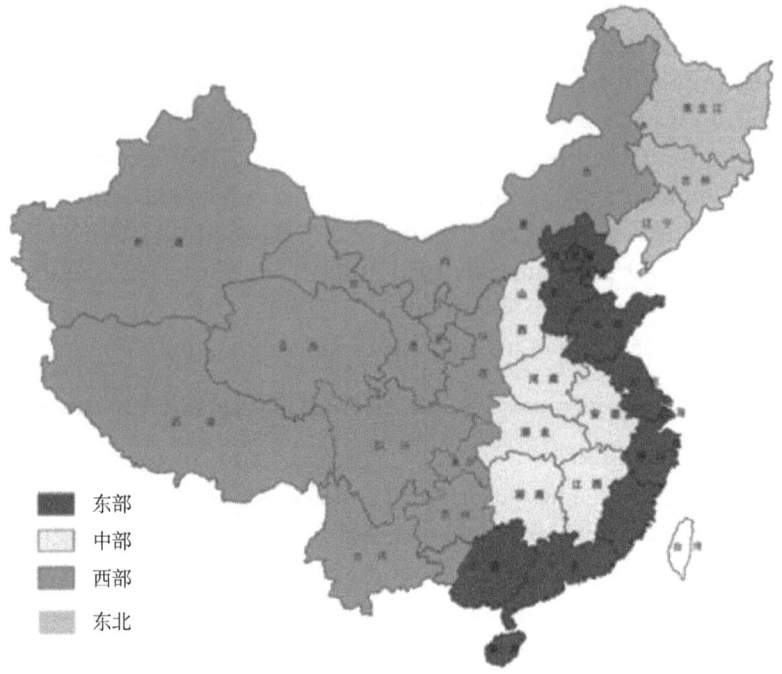

Figure 1-4 Regional divisions in China: eastern, western and central regions

(5) Huge regional disparities in urbanization

Due to disparities in natural environments, social situations and economic circumstances, differences and discrepancies are striking in the urbanization of individual places. In 2012, the percentages in China's eastern, western and central regions were 56.4%, 53.4% and 44.9% respectively (see Figure 1-4). In eastern coastal regions, convenient transportation and favorable locations made it possible for them to have rapidly constructed clusters of urbanized districts marked by interlocked and agglomerated cities. For central regions, urbanized districts took shape along railway lines and expressways, though they lagged behind the eastern regions due to the negative effect of resource-oriented development. For western regions, however, plagued by backward economic and social development and coupled with a fragile eco-system, urbanization was much slower outside a few key cities that urbanized at a relatively fast rate. Moreover, confined by the previous size of cities, regional disparities in urbanization were all the more significant.

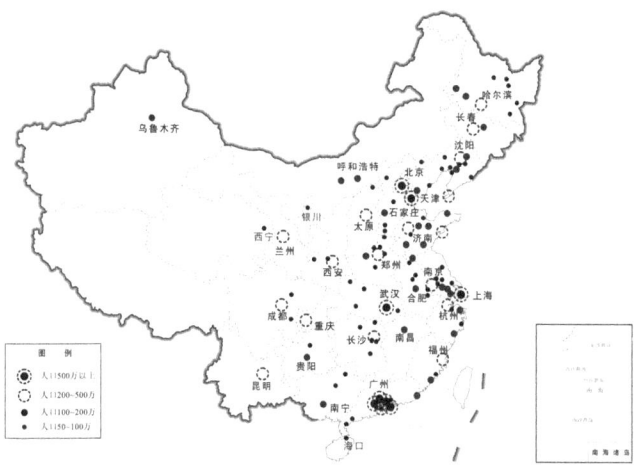

Figure 1-5 Distribution of megalopolises in China

(6) Clashes arising from urbanization: industrialization, informatization, marketization and economic globalization

In developed countries, urbanization that came along with industrialization happened hundreds of years ago. By contrast, China has been lagging behind for about 150 years. Therefore, China will definitely be confronted with intertwined conflicts and contradictions in its effort to complete the task of urbanization within decades, while the same process took almost two centuries in developed countries. China not only has to simultaneously work on urbanization and industrialization, but is faced with challenges from informatization, marketization and economic globalization. We may well say, therefore, that China's urbanization is proceeding as if within a pressure cooker of time and space. As luck would have it, urbanization in China has come about in a peaceful and stable environment, secured by a superior socialist system. Due to compressed time and space, however, many predictable and unpredictable risks, conflicts and contradictions will confront us because we shall have to address all the problems simultaneously that other countries encountered over a period of time.

II. Challenges and Problems

1. Challenges

(1) Challenges from resources and ecological environment

A. Challenges from resources

A scarcity and waste of resources, which have been impacting on the sustained progress of urbanization in China, is a hurdle that must be cleared.

These resources include water, land and energy sources, without which the process of urbanization will come to a halt. Take water, for example. Barring other negative factors such as maldistribution, China has only 2,290 cubic meters of fresh water per person. With a dramatic proliferation of the urbanized population, water supply for both homes and industry has increased significantly. To make things worse, severe pollution of both surface and underground water has widened the discrepancies between the spatial layout of urban areas and the capacity of water resources. At present, around 400 of the country's 655 cities suffer from water deficiency, and about 200 of them have been plagued by acute water shortage. The daily water deficit in urban areas across the country has hit 16 million cubic meters, with an annual shortage of about 6 billion cubic meters. The result is that water supply has to be restricted in some cities in the north.

As for land resources, conflict between the huge demand for land for urban construction and the amount available is increasingly intense, given the extreme scarcity of land resources. With the acceleration of China's urbanization, the deficiency of land resources, notably arable or cultivated land, has become stark. The preliminary result of the Second National Land Census that ran from 2001 to 2009 noted that China had only 2.026 billion mu (521,000 square miles) of arable land. This was little more than the 1.8 billion mu of cultivated land that China had been warned was necessary to sustain the bottom line of its food security or decent food supply.

Things are now looking particularly grim regarding the utilization of land in China. On the one hand, a shortage of land for urban construction is becoming the biggest problem standing in the way of a city's future development. On the other hand, the waste of land that prevails in urban construction has gravely impeded the promotion of the overall quality and normal performance of cities, brought down their load-bearing capacity at large and ultimately hampered the sound development of urbanization.

As far as energy is concerned, the challenges confronting China's urbanization arise from an energy shortfall and inefficient utilization, of which the former primarily features lack of supply to meet urban demand for energy, particularly petroleum and electricity. As urbanization proceeds, the development of heavy chemical industries, a boom in the urban population and improvements in living quality all increase demand for energy. Since 2003, acute power shortages have been experienced across the country and more than 20 provinces (or municipalities) have been forced to restrict electricity consumption. In 2009, China imported 204 million tons of oil, an increase of 13.9% on the previous year. That same year also witnessed a consumption of 2.74 billion tons of coal, an increase of 3% compared with the year before. Along with the rapid rise in energy consumption in urban areas, inefficiency has emerged as another problem. At present, the overall rate of energy utilization in China is approximately 33%, which is 10% lower than that in developed countries.

B. Challenges from the ecological environment

In the early days, China largely depended on industrialization to promote urbanization. During this time, there was an inadequate supply of sewage treatment facilities, which led to severe industrial pollution and discharge of urban pollutants. Meanwhile, the quick expansion of urbanization inflicted enormous problems in terms of solid waste pollution, water pollution, air pollution as well as traffic jams. In most cities, the huge amount of waste produced in confined industrial and residential areas outweighed the self-purification capability of the urban environment. It is only natural, therefore, that the increasingly grave pollution would precipitate a huge ecosystem predicament.

In 2008, China generated 1.901 billion tons of industrial solid wastes, an increase of nearly 1.1 billion tons compared with the amount produced in 2000. In the meantime, the output of household refuse also went up, reaching 154 million tons at a time when the treatment rate of urban household waste was only 66.8% on average. Water pollution in urban areas is closely related to industrial wastewater and domestic sewage, the latter of which has grown to become the leading cause of urban water pollution. As a result, drinking water sources are below acceptable levels in nearly half of the towns and cities across the country. Though air quality in urban areas is generally better than it was years ago, the problem is still acute. Of the 519 cities monitored in 2008, only 21 (accounting for 4% of the total) attained the primary standard, with 378 (72.8%) reaching the secondary standard, 113 (21.8%) meeting the third grade and seven (1.4%) failing to satisfy the third standard. Of the cities at prefecture level and above, 71.6% were up to par, and of the cities at county level, 85.6% reached the standard. Air pollution is particularly bad in the north and among large and super-large cities across the country as well as cities in coal-producing areas. Traffic jams are exacerbating the problem in big cities; the number of vehicles per road mile has been rising year by year, while average driving speeds have been falling.

(2) Challenges from the expansion of domestic demand

Compared with previous plans, the 12th Five-year Plan is notable for its focus on demand. The keynote of the 11th Five-year Plan was about how to promote growth, push forward technological progress and develop emerging industries, driven by a desire to improve competitiveness and productivity. The paramount idea of the 12th Five-year Plan was to stimulate domestic demand, in which urbanization played a crucial role. Urban construction, construction of infrastructural facilities and generation of urban agglomerations have created immense demand for materials. Then comes the phenomenon of migrant farmers, who represent the foundation of urbanization. In the long-run, farmers will rise to become members of the middle classes by seeking new, better-paid jobs. In this regard, urbanization sustains the expansion of the middle class. When more and more farmers settle down in cities, demand will grow, which will help develop both industry and the service sector. Urbanization, therefore, plays a central role in promoting domestic demand.

(3) Challenges from mediation of social conflicts

The second key element of the 12th Five-year Plan echoed a feature of the previous plan, namely the maintenance of social stability. The main difference between the two was that the former leant much more weight to mediating social conflicts. It was proposed in the 12th Five-year Plan that residents' incomes should grow in line with economic development, with an unstated ambition to bridge income gaps. Centering on China's urbanization, the government will work to expand the coverage of social security and, by boosting employment, adjusting public policies and helping farmers become urban residents, narrow income gaps while also bridging disparities in the supply of public goods. Urbanization should bring about an increase in employment and income of farmer-workers on the one hand, and narrow the gulf in the supply of public goods on the other. That is one of the most important aspects in addressing China's social problems.

2. Problems

(1) Inferior global competitiveness of key urban agglomerations

Viewed from a global context, key urban clusters in China have a relatively large proportion of manufacturing, though they are short of world-class manufacturing enterprises. Central cities are suffering both insufficient high-end capability and inferior development quality. Urban manufacturing industries and service sectors are, on the whole, at the low end of the international industrial chain due to their inferior development. In Beijing and Shanghai, the share of tertiary industry is now over 50%, but sectors such as international finance and cultural media are clearly underdeveloped. In terms of accounting, advertising and other consulting services, there are equally big gaps between them and the cities in developed countries. The infrastructure at an international level is inadequate and fails to satisfy the residential and entrepreneurial requirements of a high-end population.

(2) Inferior quality of human settlement

Housing conditions have yet to improve for urban residents on low incomes and migrant workers, who cannot afford to live in decent homes. Retrofits of urban squatter settlements, state-owned farms and forestry centers, as well as industrial and mining areas, are severely deficient. In general, reconstruction is arduous, ancillary facilities are insufficient and infrastructure is over-used.

Residents commonly face arduous commutes. Traffic jams are outrageous in big cities and seem to be getting worse. In super-large cities, the all-day saturation of main roads exceeds 70%. The average vehicle speed in downtown areas during rush hour is below 20 kilometers per hour. In the urban center of Shanghai, for instance, the saturation of half of all lanes is as high as 95% during rush hour and the average vehicle speed is only 10 kilometers per hour. In 2006, the average commuting time for Beijing residents was 43 minutes. In addition, the construction of integrated urban traffic networks has been slow and hub layouts are often irrational, leading to inefficiency in traffic flows because the means of transportation have been impeded. Third, the development of regional rail links is still at a primary stage, meaning that commuting between cities, industrial districts, seaports and airports is largely borne by expressways. Coordination between construction planning of highways and the development of urban agglomerations is inadequate, with the flow of the finished transport links differing considerably. Due to the rapid expansion of cities along routes built in earlier days, they have almost become inner-urban highways. Metro lines in big cities have yet to form effective networks that connect with bus routes and regional traffic, thereby impeding the operation of traffic management and organization.

Public service facilities fail to meet demand. Though educational and medical resources are rich in Beijing and other cities, services in surrounding areas are strikingly inadequate. Community-level hospitals, cultural centers, libraries, sports facilities, centers for youths and the elderly and other facilities closely bound up with the life of urban residents are scarce and suffer from a lack of routine maintenance and management funds. Service levels at social facilities are low and do not meet people's growing material and cultural needs. In the outskirts of cities and rural-urban fringe zones, social service establishments are inadequate and have failed to keep pace with demand.

Security and pollution problems are also apparent in urban areas; more than half of the cities across the country face water shortages, ageing waterworks and similar issues; the accumulated volume of urban household waste has reached 6 billion tons and will continue to grow in future at an annual rate of 4.8%, leading to the creation of towering garbage mountains around cities; air pollution is widely reported and more than half of urban residents live in foul atmospheric environments; most cities lack the capacity to resist natural disasters and urban malfunctioning is frequent thanks to climatic or human-generated causes.

(3) Small towns of low load-bearing capacities

In urban agglomerations, small towns are faced with insufficient momentum of development, indistinctive economies with local characteristics, lower levels of population aggregation and lack of scale. The number of residents in an average county town is about 80,000. Apart from the county towns, barely 400 designated townships have a population of more than 50,000, accounting for less than 3% of the total number. Planning and construction here is of an inferior quality, and the same applies to infrastructure and public services. A majority of minor towns will find it hard to bring about integrated infrastructure of urban water supply and sewage disposal as well as decent social services in commerce, science and technology, and education. This in turn makes it hard to attract population and industries, not to mention their ability to offer services to neighboring rural areas.

(4) Lack of substantial progress in overall urban-rural planning

Urban agglomerations have witnessed a clash of interest between cities and rural areas. With the expansion of urbanization, farmers who have lost land have been forced to go to cities. Much to their frustration, however, they generally find it hard to adapt to urban society. Rural-urban fringe zones are places where surplus workforces from the countryside aggregate. Migrant workers living in those places are still confronted with difficulties in areas such as housing, employment, children's education and social security.

Due to China's traditional preference for cities over the countryside, rural areas have long been overlooked in terms of overall consideration, and appropriate support and nurturing. In rural regions, there has been an under-investment in construction of infrastructure, while public service networks are not well established and social security systems have yet to be set up. When enormous surplus workforces flock to cities from the countryside, many elderly people are left to stay at home and, as a consequence, the rural population is now experiencing a downward trend in the number of working-age people. Grass-roots organizations are weakened in rural areas, which also suffer from a lack of vitality and development in agricultural activities. Much research associated with the building of a new countryside has involved discussions on village construction but little work has been done on promoting social and economic development in rural areas. Some researchers are blind to local practices and realities when they mindlessly propose the large-scale relocation of villages and residential centers.

(5) Pending changes in development theory

Although the construction of urban clusters in China has boomed in recent years, it has often been carried out blindly and in haste. In some areas, despite the fact that social and economic development has lagged, the connections between cities is not sufficiently close and the ecological environment is fragile; two or three cities, if they are relatively adjacent or are situated near water, will be rushed in an attempt to forge an urban agglomeration.

In other places, luxury and extravagance is pursued in urban development and construction. Some cities spend large amounts on iconic or landmark projects that are huge profile, large in scale and highly energy-consuming. Aside from being out of tune with the overall style of the cities, the projects are expensive to maintain and operate and are typically under-utilized Many other cities take a keen interest in building man-made water views or landscapes and some have gone so far as to construct vast artificial lakes in the northwest of the country where water resources are scarce. Some mountainous cities, with no regard to the peculiar topographical features of the location, decide to roll out extensive rectangular or chessboard-styled urban layouts while the establishment of public services and amenities closely bound with the life of urban-rural residents are under-invested. According to a survey conducted by Renmin University of China, despite the extra investment in urban construction and the substantial results achieved by local governments, residents' satisfaction with cities is strikingly deteriorating.

Uncalled-for expansion is widely found in industrial development zones when some cities exploit the land for industrial purposes. More often than not, an industrial development zone would occupy an area of 100 square kilometers and more. In some places, industrial parks are so disproportionate in number as to have triggered vicious competition, with the consequence that the cost for development has been forced down and excess production capacity has resulted.

III. New Urbanization Strategies and Solutions

It was noted for the first time in a report to the 18th National Congress of the CPC that new urbanization is both a vehicle for building an affluent society in an all-round way and a focus for changing the growth mode of the economy. The characteristics of new urbanization in a Chinese context are that it is intensive, intelligent, green and low-carbon. It is based on the idea of a scientific outlook on development and adheres to the principles of being people-centric and preserving the culture and environment, while simultaneously pushing forward industrialization, informatization, urbanization and modernization of agriculture in order to promote the quality and level of urbanization, urban-rural integration and coordinated development between regions.

1. Regular Migration of Rural Population to Urban Areas

The migration of rural residents to towns and cities is not entirely a market process. Government policies are needed to provide guidance and intervention in order to effect a well-organized transfer. Besides, the tools for implementing the policies are equally necessary. The policies for an orderly shift of rural people to urban areas should be worked out as follows.

First, those who enter cities could be grouped into types. For floaters or floating peasant-workers, a two-way flow policy is suggested, which means that they can retain their dual status or identities as both workers and peasants. This means their legal interests such as pay, working hours, official holidays and safety protection are secured by law. For those who have stable jobs and residences in cities, conditions should be created for them to become urban residents, after which they will be entitled to the same rights and obligations as local residents. For rural folk whose contracted land has been requisitioned by the government due to urbanization, they will have to be transformed into or acknowledged as urban residents for whom the municipal government should offer employment assistance, technical training, unemployment insurance and subsistence allowances. Rural residents should be encouraged to come to settle down in small towns and small and medium-sized cities. Super-large cities should center on industrial restructuring to gradually bring into being a mechanism by which they can harness excessive population growth by means of economic measures.[3]

Second, studies on predicting occupational demand and laws of population mobility should be underpinned. Information systems of occupational demand and population migration should be established by both the state and local governments so that information about occupational demand will be monitored and provided in line with the needs of industrialization, economic development, urbanization and the construction of national defense.

Third, policies for managing census registers should be reformed and a unified system for managing urban-rural household registers should be progressively worked out.

Fourth, population transfer and industrial restructuring should be integrated as a whole so as to optimize demographic structures, reshape the pattern of population distribution and ultimately create coordination and balance between population, employment, resources, the ecological environment and other parameters.

2. Well-organized Spatial Patterns for Urbanization

Most important of all, big cities should be allowed to develop fully so that their leading role can be deployed in driving development. As is widely accepted, it has been one of the laws in urbanization for big cities to take the lead in development. At the initial and intermediate stages of urbanization, free expansion and full development of big cities play a major role in upgrading the level and quality of urbanization and it is arguably the primary prerequisite for the completion of urbanization and formation of a relatively perfect urban system. Without free and full development of big cities, the idea to first bring about the extensive development of small and medium-sized cities is but a fantasy conceived of by those who seek in vain to go beyond the development stage.

---

[3] See *The 11th Five-year Plan for National Economic and Social Development of the People's Republic China*. Beijing: People's Publishing House, 2006

Second, urban clusters should play leading roles in pushing forward urbanization so that they will help create metropolitan regions or megalopolises and urban clusters before boosting their further development. On this basis, China will gradually establish a sustainable and highly coordinated spatial framework of urbanization with the coastal regions and Beijing-Guangzhou-Harbin Railway as the longitudinal axis, the Yangtze River and Longhai Railway as the horizontal axis, and a significant number of urban clusters as the main body surrounding which other cities and towns are distributed in a scattered pattern that are regularly interspersed with permanent arable land and ecological zones. Megalopolises that emerged up to two decades ago have long been taken as advanced forms in the development of cities. They have acted as 'dynamos' that spearhead economic growth in the modern market economy, often occupying a central position in innovation and the accumulation of wealth. A megalopolis centers on one or several big cities around which are aggregated many small or small and medium-sized towns, covering an area that can be as vast as tens of thousands of square kilometers. In 1976, Jean Gottmann, the well-known French geographer, observed that six world-level megalopolises had by then taken shape across the globe, the Yangtze River Delta being among them. Things have moved on since then. At present, the GDP generated by the three megalopolises in the US and Japan account for 65% and 69% respectively of their national totals. It is predicted that 12 megalopolises will exist in China by 2020. Today, it already has three megalopolises – the Beijing-Tianjin-Hebei, Yangtze River Delta and Pearl River Delta megalopolises – and their combined GDP now accounts for 38% of the national total. For the time being, the three megalopolises should continue to play leading roles in coordinating responsibilities and complementing each other's advantages between cities within the metropolitan regions so that their collective competitiveness will be enhanced. As for the regions that are basically qualified for developing into urban clusters, they should work to intensify coordinated planning with large and super-large cities as locomotives and give full play to central cities so as to bring into being some new urban clusters that occupy less land, offer more employment opportunities, are capable of pooling more factors and have a more rational distribution of population.

Finally, towns and small and medium-sized cities should be guided to develop intensively in cultivating special industries according to their own characteristics so that their comparative advantages will become apparent. In regions where no urban agglomeration can occur due to their thinly-scattered populations and deficient resources, they should be encouraged to develop around existing cities, county towns and well-qualified designate townships to build them into centers that aggregate economy, population and public services. As striking as big cities are, most urban populations across the globe have been living in towns and small and medium-sized cities. In this light, substantial measures should be taken for expanding the scale of small towns to facilitate the aggregation process.

3. Efficient and Economic Use of Resources for Eco-protection

First, the government should strengthen its policy guidance for, and studies on, energy-saving technologies connected with construction, transportation and other key sources of energy consumption. Measures should be worked out for standard systems, supervision and implementation that aim to promote environmental protection and reduce the consumption of energy, land, water and raw materials. Energy and land-saving construction projects should be factored into the index framework and system of land for urban-rural construction. Research should be conducted into the index system of designing residential communities and isolated buildings in cities as well as the control index system for residential construction planning in rural areas, both systems having to be strictly implemented. The thermal insulation system of structures currently in use should be improved and the application of solar and other renewable energies in construction should be accelerated. Computation systems for the life-cycle cost of buildings should be established and strengthened, and effective reward mechanisms must be formulated for energy saving, water conservation and waste reclamation. Investigation of urban water-supply networks and household water instruments should be underpinned in order to reduce leakage. Studies on fuel-efficient vehicles should be reinforced and the application of clean and renewable energies should be promoted. In single-center cities, public transport should be given top priority and carpooling should be encouraged. Rapid, convenient and comfortable public transport systems, including exclusive bus lanes, should be set up. In super-large cities, congestion charging could be adopted. Supporting policies should be stipulated, cooperation agreements should be made in industrial sectors, and demand-side management ought to be implemented with legal, power pricing and funding support. Security mechanisms should be established for the market of renewable energy generation in order to stimulate investment in renewable energies and promote technological progress in developing and utilizing renewable energies with the guarantee of stable and sustainable measures.

Second, construction of eco-cities should be advocated. Urban areas should be taken as compound ecosystems composed of society, the economy and environment in planning, construction and management. Ecological cost or natural capital should be included in economic analysis and policy making of governments at all levels. The protection of urban ecosystems and promotion of urban environmental quality as well residents' living conditions should be listed among the key indicators for evaluating urban construction and performances of local governments.

Third, modes of production and consumption should be changed. Urban areas consume and discharge huge quantities of materials every day. Take Zhuhai in Guangdong province, for example. In 2000, the city had an average daily demand for 5,820 tons of coal, 1,595 tons of fuel, 600,000 tons of water and 1,127 tons of food. Each day it discharges 602 tons of industrial solid waste, 300,000 tons of waste water and 1,000 tons of garbage. Unless the modes of production and consumption in cities are changed, it will not be possible to adequately address the problems of wasting resources and environmental pollution simply by means of advanced technologies and infrastructure construction. In this light, we must work out policies for product recycling and reclamation, encourage energy- and resource-saving products, promote public transport, propagate and appeal to saving energy, change lifestyles and entertainment, and work to integrate protection of the environment and sanitation with economic planning and policies. With the assistance of the market mechanism and economic measures, we will be able to establish clean and ecological cities.

Fourth, land-use planning and policies adapted to the market economy should be formulated. For example, maximum and minimum plot rates should be nailed down for industrial land. For residential land, additional charges should be imposed on those developing land at low volumes and those holding multiple homes in order to avert the wasting of land and excessive use of land. In line with the goals of urban economic and social development during a given period and by means of investigation and developing prediction, directions and guidelines for developing underground space should be proposed according to the planning for ground or surface construction for the purpose of determining the goal, function, scale and layout of urban underground space as well as the overall arrangement of all underground facilities. Super-large cities should take the lead in working out planning for utilizing underground space.

Fifth, pilot tests should be conducted with the help of foreign practices to economize and recover investment in energy-saving by means of internal contracts. This policy, which aims to address problems relevant to the mechanism generated in the start-up of capital and effective recovery of capital, is exercisable inside a mega unit. If the economic analysis and recommendations about energy saving wins the stamp of approval by superior departments, then the mega unit will be entitled to set up the project and enter into a contract with its subordinate executing entities. After that, the capital will start to go into the energy-saving project. Upon completion of the project, energy costs will be reduced and these savings will be returned to the unit. Such projects may include heating-supply control, ventilation, daylighting, wall and roof insulation, protection of football fields, street lamps, automatic temperature control, water saving and cogeneration. Easy to implement, these projects can address problems related to varied channels of expenditure on and investment in energy, but also significantly reduce users' costs.

4. Reinforcing Management of Urban Planning

First, planning for the size and layout of cities should be adapted not only to the local land and water resources, environmental capability, geological structure and other natural bearing capacities, but also to local economic development, employment space, infrastructure and public service capabilities.

Second, urban planning and construction should be improved as a whole. Protection of urban water sources must be reinforced and water supply facilities should be adequately established. Cities short of water should moderately rationalize the scale of construction and must be deterred from developing water-intensive industries and artificial water landscapes. Cities suffering from overuse of groundwater should resist further exploitation to avoid land subsidence. Segmentation between sectors and regions should be subjugated in constructing urban roads, waterworks and drainage systems, telecom and cable TV, as well as in energy and environmental protection. Coordinated construction should be executed based on unified planning so as to reduce mindless removal and reconstruction. A city's disaster-prevention and mitigation capacities should be reinforced, as should emergency response and recovery capabilities. The legal interests of relocated households must be guaranteed in the regular renovation of dilapidated houses and 'urban villages'. The planning, designing and building of urban areas must be carried out in a way that is sensitive to history and traditional culture, highlighting distinctive features, protecting national characteristics, and preserving cultural relics and scenic resources. The implementation of urban planning must be supervised and the integrated administration of cities should be pushed forward so that the overall urban management will be enhanced.

Third, division or segregation between sectors in planning should change. The relationships between regional planning, land-use planning, urban planning and other primary categories of spatial planning are in urgent need of adjustment and clarification Urban and land-use planning work should be incorporated within the territory of cities and, in the meantime, integrated with the planning of social and economic development. The government should straighten out structural relationships between relevant functional departments, reinforce the legal framework and bring into being a national planning system that is unified and strong in controlling and regulation.

Fourth, the mechanism of urban-rural planning, in accordance with the *Urban and Rural Planning Law*, should be brought into full play by promoting the planning of the main functional regions or development priority zones so that strategic planning for cross-regional spatial development will be followed.

Fifth, village populations have fallen as many households have relocated and massive homesteads have been discarded after farmers have left their hometowns for cities. Therefore, the government should reintegrate the establishments in rural areas, rationalize the layout of rural settlements and facilitate the transfer of homesteads left behind by farmers in towns according to law so that the land will be protected for fairer use.

5. Developing Industry-financed Agriculture and Urban-sustained Rural Areas

Concerted and coordinated urban-rural development is central to the accomplishment of sustainable urbanization. At present, the Chinese government has publicized its new thinking on social and economic development: to have industry nurture agriculture and cities support the countryside so as to achieve the concerted and coordinated development of them all. The government, in an effort to establish a stable and gradual growth mechanism of agricultural input, has resolved to restructure the pattern of national income distribution and is determined to carry out a substantial preferential policy for agriculture, the countryside and farmers in its financial expenditure and investment in fixed assets based on current agricultural inputs. That means that the government is determined to bring to an end its trajectory of development at the initial stage of industrialization when agriculture was relied on as the viable source of government revenue to supply accumulated capital for industry; from now on, agriculture and the rural sector will be eligible for government support. To this end, the Chinese government will strive to accomplish the following things:

First, it will further reinforce investment in rural infrastructure, bring small and medium-scale rural infrastructure construction into the scope of government investment in its capital construction of all levels, and increase its investment in irrigation and water conservation as well as country roads and other small-scale rural infrastructure.

Second, it will improve the security mechanism for rural compulsory educational expenditure financed in large part by the government, further increase its investment in the rural public health system, upgrade the assistance system for rural vulnerable groups, enhance the coverage of social security in rural areas, strengthen investment in agricultural research, intensify scientific and technological innovation in agriculture, and establish an agricultural technical promotion system, so as to promote the development of science and technology, education, culture and medical services in rural areas on the one hand, and improve employment opportunities for farmers on the other.

Third, it will conduct studies and work out a new land-use pattern for both construction and agriculture during the process of urbanization and in the meantime formulate supporting policies designed to increase charges for the paid use of newly-added construction land. While tightening up the collection, management, use and supervision of land-leasing fees, it will adjust the distribution structure of land revenue and permit peasants whose land is expropriated to have a share in projects as shareholders or leaseholders of the estates of contracted land so that they can enjoy the value-added payoff of land. Based on the returned 15% of land-leasing fees invested in rural infrastructure and social projects, the return rate of land-leasing fees will be increased step by step and further invested in rural infrastructure and social projects.

Fourth, the government will improve urban employment policies in an effort to create more job opportunities for peasants in cities. It will carry out reemployment training programs for peasant-workers with the government and enterprises sharing the costs and gradually establish a unified urban-rural labor market. It will spare no efforts in finding solutions to the problems relating to the schooling of migrant workers' children, public health, cultural life, social security and other issues so as to establish an institutional environment that is accessible to farmers. In the final analysis, the government will ultimately change the urban-rural dual structure.

Chapter 2

Development of Urban-rural Planning in China

I. Urban-rural Planning in China since 1949

After the founding of the PRC in 1949, modern urban planning has witnessed many ups and downs, as indeed has Chinese society. In general, we can split this period in two, with 1978 as the dividing point. This chapter aims to look back on this time and summarize the evolution of China's urban planning before and after the reform and opening-up process.

1. Urban-rural Planning Prior to Reform and Opening Up

(1) Initial stage of urban planning (1949-1952)

Before 1949, cities in China typically had the characteristics of a semi-colonial and semi-feudal society. Most inland cities and towns had a poorly developed industrial sector and appalling living conditions; at the time, there was a lack of both modern industries and modern municipal works or public facilities. By contrast, the big colonial cities along the coast were more commercially developed and often had quite advanced municipal facilities, although divisions and conflicts between social groups were alarming, with slums and western-style houses standing in stark contrast. Take Shanghai, for example. In the 1930s, the 'Paris of the Orient' was widely known as the world's fifth largest city and a prosperous international metropolis, where the Bund, crowded with people and vehicles, displayed the grandest western architecture (see Figure 2-1). In contrast to the prosperity and modernity of the foreign concessions, however, were the dwellings of the poor. Along the Zhaojiabang River, for example, was a well-known shanty settlement (see Figure 2-2) that was jam-packed with a mosaic of ramshackle shacks, tiny gambling houses known as 'crawling dragons', bamboo scaffolding projecting over the water, shabby boats on the river and dilapidated sheds under bridges that were occupied by tens of thousands of paupers.

Figure 2-1 The Bund in Shanghai (1930s)

Figure 2-2 Shanty settlement in Zhaojiabang, Shanghai (1930s)

During the economic recovery following the ravages of war, the priority was to quickly restore devastated factories and enterprises and in the meantime construct more plants and businesses. One such company was Anshan Integrated Iron and Steel Works in Liaoning province. With regards to urban construction, the government, due to its limited economic capability, was only in a position to focus on the renovation of some shanty settlements in certain big cities so that the housing and living conditions at grassroots level would be improved; a relatively well-known example involved the reconstruction of Longxu Ditch in Beijing. As was the case with the Zhaojiabang shanty settlement in Shanghai, the region along the ditch was then known as the most poverty-stricken place in Beijing. Moreover, the water channel was heavily polluted and foul smelling all the year round. After the founding of the New China, the reconstruction project conducted in this area was completed within only three months.

With the recovery and focus on city construction, urban planning also got under way. Beginning in 1950, research institutions related to urban planning and construction management offices were established one after another in big cities.[4] In September 1952, the central government convened the National Urban Construction Symposium, at which it formally proposed that city planning must be highlighted. After that, it set up urban construction institutions and reinforced its leadership in city construction.

After three years' adaptation, recovery and development, China's urban planning and construction sectors started to embark on a new stage, its target being the development of industrial cities.

(2) Import and development of 'Soviet-mode' urban planning (1953-1957)

This phase witnessed the formulation and implementation of China's First Five-year Plan for the national economy. During the period, 'Soviet-mode' planning was imported at a time when China was in pressing need for a city planning system as it carried out large-scale industrial construction centered on 156 priority projects with help from the former Soviet Union, and to properly address their relationships with existing cities.

The 'Soviet model' conceived of urban planning as the materialization and extension of national economic planning. In fact, the architects of the former Soviet Union's urban planning simply held that the features of socialist cities could simply boil down to productivity or productiveness,

---

[4] Leon Hoa. *Reconstruction of China: Urban Planning within Three Decades* [M]. Translated by Li Ying. Beijing: SDX Joint Publishing Company, 2006, page 28

believing that cities must undertake industrial production and that the main advantages of socialist cities and their planning involved planned production and the nationalization of land.

In the early years of the PRC, the formulators of China's urban planning adopted the entire catalogue of procedures and methods laid down by the former Soviet Union. In 1956, preparation and modification of the *Provisional Regulations for Formulation of Urban Planning*, the first technical law on city planning in China, was completed with the participation of Kravchuk, leader of the expert group from the former Soviet Union, counselor of China's Construction Commission and expert on urban planning. The Provisional Regulations have had a long-lasting influence on China's urban planning and construction, even to the present day.

Having drawn so much on the practices of the former Soviet Union, including the whole category of urban planning theories and methods aligned with the system of planning, China's city planning and construction at the time featured a rigid planned economy and a touch of 'classical formalism' that highlighted plane composition, stereoscopic dimension, symmetry of axes, radiating roads, facing views, and double-curbside blocks and street views (see Figure 2-3). In addition, there was a time when economic efficiency was ignored due to its over-pursuit of scale, area, novelty, speed and standard in urban construction.

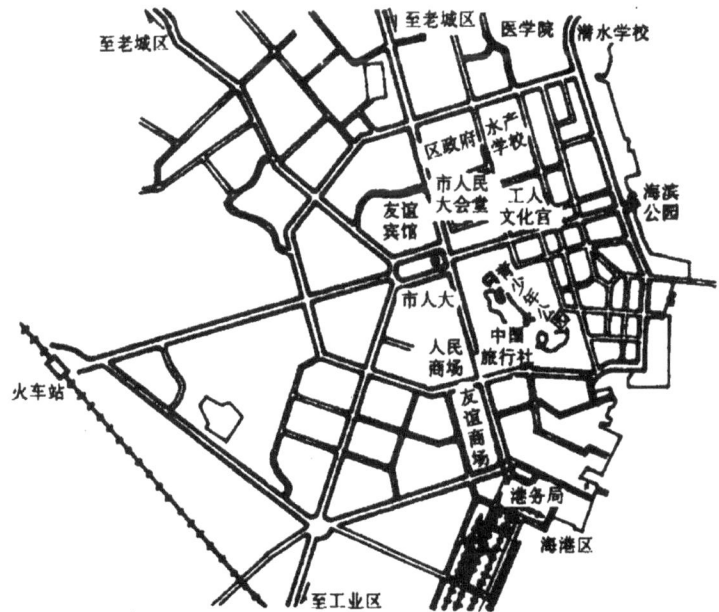

Figure 2-3 Structure of the ring-shaped new urban area in Xiashan, Zhanjiang

(3) Urban planning turmoil and disruption phase (1958-1977)

This period lasted for as long as two decades. However, because of the considerable fluctuation in politics and the economy, city planning and construction was thrown into turmoil and even disrupted. This was particularly the case after the start of the Cultural Revolution in 1966, when urban planning was severely impacted. Normal operations were suspended, institutions closed down, professional teams disbanded, urban planning education at colleges and universities was canceled, and literature damaged; the professional contingent were left in an even more fragile and unstable condition. The outcome was that urban development ground to a standstill, urban planning became virtually stagnant, city construction and management were thrown into semi-anarchy, places of interest and green landscapes were usurped or vandalized, and unauthorized buildings sprouted everywhere; the chaotic urban layout caused irreparable damage and left behind a mass of intractable legacies.

2. Urban-rural Planning after 1978

When the Cultural Revolution came to a stop at the end of 1976, China started to embark on a new historical period of development. The convening of the Third Plenary Session of the 11th Central Committee of the CPC, more than anything else, brought about an even more profound change for China's economy and society; urban planning and construction entered a new stage of development. This period could be further subdivided into four stages as follows.

(1) Restoration of urban planning (1978-1980)

The Third Conference on Urban Development held in 1978 reviewed the practices and lessons in urban planning over the previous three decades and proposed that city planning should be restored and strengthened. In October 1980, the National Construction Committee held the National Work Conference on Urban Planning, where delegates joined in a discussion about how city planning should adapt to the goals of the four modernizations in terms of: economic and social development; the overall position and functions of urban planning in national construction; and the responsibilities of mayors in the planning, construction and management of their cities, discussed and passed the legislation on urban planning. The conference formulated the guideline that the size and scale of big cities should be controlled, that medium-sized cities should be developed moderately, and that the development of small cities should be given priority. It was urged that both the general and detailed urban programs of all cities must be worked out by the end of 1982. Having helped straighten out the ideas on city planning, the conference was a landmark event in the historical development of urban planning in modern China.

(2) Legalization of urban planning (1980s)

During the 1980s, master urban planning work was carried out across the country for the benefit of urban construction. By 1986, 96% of planned cities and 85% of counties and townships nationwide had completed their general planning for construction, of which 80% had passed approval. The drawing up and approval of the second wave of urban planning underlined that China had entered a period of urban construction and development in line with the planning scientifically worked out.[5]

On December 26, 1989, the Standing Committee of the Seventh National People's Congress passed the *Urban Planning Law of the PRC*. This identified by means of legislation the position and role of urban planning in national construction, teased out the various relations in the compiling and management of urban planning, defined its contents and methods, and highlighted the procedure and jurisdiction of its management, so that the authority and status of urban planning were secured, with the formulation and implementation of it being guaranteed by law. That truly constituted a milestone in the establishment and management of China's urban planning, signifying that the country had embarked on the trajectory of urban governance according to law in its city planning and construction.

Special Column 2-1 The first legislation on urban planning

On December 26, 1989, the National People's Congress passed the *Urban Planning Law of the PRC*, the country's first state law on modern city planning. The law is composed of 46 articles in six chapters and its contents are as follows: (1) general provisions: limitations, relevant definitions and stipulations on institutions; (2) formulation of the plan for a city: organizations and principles for the compiling of city planning, stages, requirements, approval and modification; (3) development of new urban areas and redevelopment of existing urban areas: principles for the planning

---

[5] Dong Jianhong. *Urban History of China* (third edition) [M]. Beijing: China Architecture & Building Press, 2004, page 400

of new and old districts, and the layout of some important facilities; (4) implementation of city planning: promulgation of city planning, 'one proposal and two permits' (see Section 4 of this chapter for contents) and relevant development control; (5) legal liability; (6) supplementary provisions.

— Excerpted from *Urban History of China* by Dong Jianhong, Beijing: China Architecture & Building Press, July 2004, pages 400-401

(3) Reform of urban planning (1990s-2007)

In the 1990s, particularly after Deng Xiaoping delivered his Southern Tour speeches and the decision to establish a socialist market economic system was made at the 14th National Congress of the CPC, city construction started a stage of faster development. In the meantime, however, with an undue emphasis on things large and foreign, huge projects, squares and European-style projects proliferated across the country. Several cities boasted implausibly that they would build an international metropolis, 'villa areas' and 'development zones' of all descriptions were everywhere, as the Urban Planning Law was flouted and the abuse and unauthorized acquisition of land went on unchecked, along with ecological damage and a waste of capital. In May 1996, the State Council, in order to quell the chaos and disorder in city planning, promulgated the *Notice on Strengthening City Planning*. The Notice stipulated that the 80 large cities whose non-agricultural population totaled more than 500,000 must submit their comprehensive planning to the State Council for examination and approval. In line with this, the Ministry of Construction laid out regulations on the new wave of comprehensive urban planning, demanding that the size of cities must be brought under strict control, that the goal of development for modernized cities must be well studied and established, that the optimization of industrial structure must be highlighted, that the setup of cities must be readjusted and that macroeconomic regulation must be strengthened.

By the end of the 1990s, the third round of comprehensive planning for planned cities had largely been compiled. In modifying urban planning, market economic theories and laws were widely applied. At the same time, people began to explore in practice compiling methods for urban planning adapted to the requirements of the development of the market economy in their stress on the guidance of regulatory detailed planning in developing land. In Shenzhen and other cities, with the establishment of a statutory planning system,[6] technical documents of urban planning were turned into local regulations after being approved legally and urban planning therefore became a public policy. In the meantime, computers, networks, remote sensing and other new technologies were widely applied in the making and management of city planning. During this period, the role of urban planning was elevated within the context of the socialist market economy, while administration according to the law was held in higher regard.

(4) Integrated urban-rural planning (after 2008)

Since the start of reform and opening up, the construction of a legal system in China's urban-rural planning had lagged behind the rapid progress in urbanization. Prior to 2008, the legal system as a whole in urban-rural planning could be generalized as 'one law with one regulation'. 'One law' refers to the Urban Planning Law, while 'one regulation' is the *Management Regulation on Planning and Construction of Villages and Towns* issued by the State Council in June 1993. The detachment between cities and the countryside in the making and implementation of planning that has resulted in a lack of coherence and coordination in urban-rural planning was out of step with the boom in China's economy and society. As urbanization progressed, many villages and small towns became designated towns in which planning and management are hard to coordinate because they involve two legal systems. Even in the economically developed coastal region, many areas are untouched by the coverage of urban-rural planning. The development of urbanization has stimulated a need to perfect the existing legal system for urban-rural planning.

On October 28, 2007, based on the practices of the Urban Planning Law, the *Management Regulation on Planning and Construction of Villages and Towns*, and the management of China's urban-rural planning after reform and opening up, the *Urban and Rural Planning Law of the PRC* was promulgated at the 30th meeting of the Standing Committee of the 10th

---

[6] The statutory plan was drawn up annually by sectors responsible for urban planning in line with both global and zoning urban plans. It laid down for districts within the zone detailed stipulations and regulations on the nature of land use, intensity of development, auxiliary facilities, traffic networks, urban designing and others. In making its zoning program and detailed planning, Shenzhen included the preparation of a statutory plan with the principal aim of further clarifying the plan for the nature of land use, intensity of development and auxiliary facilities within each district. The statutory plan took legal effect with the approval of the Municipal Planning Committee and no-one was entitled to make an unauthorized change. With regard to the making of its statutory plan, Shenzhen used to consult with the public; the transparency of its urban planning was increased when opinions from the public were adopted in modifying the statutory plan by the municipal planning sector. The statutory plan helped strengthen the spirit of legality in making urban planning, as well as increase public understanding of and participation in urban planning

National People Congress. It took effect on January 1, 2008. In this law, the formulation, implementation, modification, supervision and liability of planning, particularly the making and carrying out of the planning of townships and villages, were stipulated at length.

Special Column 2-2 Improvements in the Urban and Rural Planning Law compared with the Urban Planning Law

Qiu Baoxing, vice minster of China's Ministry of Housing and Urban-rural Construction, notes that improvements in the Urban and Rural Planning Law, compared with the Urban Planning Law, can be summarized in seven aspects.[7]

First, in the Urban and Rural Planning Law, the dual urban-rural legal system previously formulated has been integrated.

Second, with respect to the guidelines on which they are based, the Urban Planning Law draws attention to 'guiding construction', while the Urban and Rural Planning Law highlights resource conservation. From compilation to implementation, the Urban and Rural Planning Law stresses the preservation and protection of farmland, natural resources, cultural heritage and places of interest, and works to exercise various protection measures of all resources with planning areas.

Third, with regard to methods and approaches, the Urban Planning Law attaches importance to planning and approval while the Urban and Rural Planning Law lays stress on execution and supervision of planning. To reinforce supervision, the Urban and Rural Planning Law specifically included an extra chapter on supervision and examination that emphasizes superintendence by the National People's Congress, the public and superior departments.

Fourth, the subjects of liability shall not be penalized in case of breaching planning in the Urban Planning Law, while accountability is clearly specified and self-discipline of departments in charge of urban-rural planning is reinforced in the Urban and Rural Planning Law. For instance, relevant administrative liabilities have been well defined for those directly in charge of and responsible for the commission or approval of commission of an illegal act, and in cases

---

[7] This part of the discussion largely referred to *Urban and Rural Planning Law in the Eyes of Qiu Baoxing* by Liu Hua, China Construction, 2008 (2), page 14

of an abuse of power, malpractice or favoritism that constitutes a crime, criminal responsibility shall be affixed.

Fifth, the Urban Planning Law underlines the role and function of planning departments while the Urban and Rural Planning Law gives priority to public participation and social supervision. For example, in line with the Urban and Rural Planning Law, a notice shall be announced for at least 30 days prior to the approval of urban-rural planning. The departments responsible for working out urban-rural planning shall take full account of expert and public opinions and have the reasons for the adoption of opinions attached to the materials to be submitted for approval. Before submitting for approval, village planning shall be decided after adequate discussion at villagers' meetings. The approved urban-rural planning shall be made known to society in a timely manner, apart from those matters that should not be made public according to laws and administrative regulations.

Sixth, the Urban and Rural Planning Law has further improved the handling mechanism for unauthorized construction and set down, according to law, administrative penalties and coercive measures for them to be ordered to stop building, to be rectified within the deadline, to have a penalty imposed on them, to be dismantled within the time limit, and for the property to be confiscated. In the meantime, it is stipulated that the local people's government shall oblige the departments concerned to seal the construction sites and conduct compulsory demolition if the relevant parties fail to stop building or dismantling within the time limit.

Seventh, with the acceleration of urbanization, no planning will be able to accommodate the rapid change of urbanization without adequate resilience. To this end, the Urban and Rural Planning Law accentuates the modification of planning and has specifically included an extra chapter in which the essentials and procedures for modification are clarified.

II. Designers and Executives of Urban-rural Planning in China

The administrative system of urban-rural planning is associated with the establishment of planning administrations at all levels as well as the right and obligation in mapping out and implementing urban-rural planning.

In accordance with China's Urban and Rural Planning Law, the Ministry of Housing and Urban-rural Construction, the urban-rural planning administrative agency under the State Council, is in full charge of the country's urban-rural planning. The urban-rural administrative departments of local governments above county level are responsible for urban-rural planning within their administrative regions. The urban-rural planning administrations of all levels play the overarching role in developing (inclusive of compiling and approving) and implementing the planning.

1. Administration and Establishment of Urban-rural Planning

(1) Formulation

   A. The competent department in charge of urban-rural planning under the State Council shall, together with other departments under the State Council, organize the establishment of the national urban system planning.

   B. The people's government of a province or autonomous region shall organize the establishment of its provincial urban system planning.

   C. The people's government of a city shall organize the establishment of its overall planning.

   D. The county people's government shall organize the establishment of overall planning of the town where the county people's government is located. The overall planning of any other town shall be established by the people's government of that town.

   E. The formulation of regulatory detailed planning of a city shall be organized by the competent sector under the city people's government in conformity with the requirements of its city planning.

   F. The regulatory detailed planning of a town shall be established by the people's government of the town in accordance with the requirements of the town's master planning; the regulatory detailed planning of the town where the county people's government is located shall be established by the competent urban-rural planning department under the government of the same level in conformity with the requirements of the comprehensive planning.

   G. The site detailed planning of a key district shall be drawn up by the competent urban-rural planning department under the city or county people's government jointly with the people's government of the town.

H. The planning of the township or administrative village shall be established by the people's government of the townships or the administrative village.

(2) Examination and approval

A. The national urban system planning shall be filed by the competent department of urban and rural planning under the State Council, with the State Council exercising examination and approval.

B. The provincial urban system planning shall be filed by the people's government of a province or autonomous region, with the State Council exercising examination and approval.

C. The overall planning of a municipality directly under the central government shall be filed by the people's government of the municipality with the State Council for examination and approval. The overall planning of a city where the provincial or autonomous region people's government is located, or which is specified by the State Council, shall be filed with the State Council for examination and approval after it is examined and approved by the provincial or autonomous region people's government. The overall planning of any other city shall be filed by the people's government of the city, with the provincial or autonomous region people's government exercising examination and approval.

D. The overall planning of a town where the county people's government is located shall be filed by the county people's government with the people's government at the next higher level exercising examination and approval. The overall planning of any other town shall be filed by the people's government of that town, with the people's government at the next higher level exercising examination and approval.

E. The people's government of a town shall, in accordance with the requirements of the overall planning of that town, organize the establishment of a regulatory detailed planning and file the planning with the people's government at the next higher level for examination and approval. The regulatory detailed planning of the town where the county people's government is located shall be established by the competent department of urban and rural planning under the county people's government in accordance with the overall planning of the town, and be filed with the standing committee of the people's congress at the same level and the people's government at the next higher level for archival purpose upon the approval of the county people's government.

F. The planning of a township or administrative village shall be submitted by the people's government of the township or town to the people's government of the next higher level for approval. The planning of a natural village shall be discussed and agreed upon at the villagers' meeting or villagers' representative meeting prior to submission for examination and approval.

G. The provincial urban system planning established by the people's government of a province or an autonomous region or the overall planning established by the people's government of a municipality or county shall, before it is submitted to the people's government at the next higher level for examination and approval, be deliberated on by the standing committee of the people's congress at the same level, and the deliberation opinions of the members of the standing committee shall be submitted to the people's government at the same level for consideration.

The overall planning of a town established by the people's government of the town shall, before it is submitted to the people's government at the next higher level for examination and approval, be first deliberated on by the people's congress of the town, and the deliberation opinions of the deputies shall be submitted to the people's government at the same level for consideration.

When filing a provincial urban system planning, a city overall planning or a town overall planning for examination and approval, the organ establishing the planning shall file the deliberation opinions of the members of the standing committee of the people's congress at the same level or the deputies to the people's congress of the town as well as the changes in the planning made in accordance with the opinions.

H. Before filing an urban or rural planning for examination and approval, the organ establishing it shall announce the draft of the planning and collect opinions from experts and the general public by way of argumentation, hearing or other ways. The draft shall be announced for at least 30 days.

2. Administration and Implementation of Urban-rural Planning

During the implementation phase, the competent administrative department responsible for urban planning is supposed to carry out the following duties: to approve land use and construction projects, to supervise, inspect and finally accept completed projects, to impose penalties, and to conduct an administrative review or reconsideration.

The Urban and Rural Planning Law authorizes all competent local urban-rural planning departments to examine and approve land use and construction projects within the planning areas. All competent local administrative departments in charge of urban-rural planning are supposed to enter into the checking and final acceptance of the completed key construction projects within the planning areas and are entitled to supervise and inspect construction projects within the planning areas to confirm their conformity to the requirements of the planning.

All competent local administrative departments responsible for planning have the right to impose penalties on illegal construction. If the disputing party remains unconvinced with the administrative penalty, it is allowed to ask the administrative department at a higher level in charge of planning for an administrative review within the time limit or immediately sue at the People's Court.

The implementation of planning, therefore, largely rests with local competent administrative departments in charge of urban-rural planning and the administrative sector or sectors of a higher level are only responsible for administrative reviews or reconsiderations.

Special Column 2-3 Supervision and inspection in complementing urban-rural planning

As a centerpiece of the management of urban-rural planning and a major means to guarantee that it is worked out scientifically and seriously, supervision and inspection runs throughout the whole process of formulation and implementation of urban-rural planning. To reinforce surveillance on urban-rural planning so as to ensure it is taken seriously, an extra chapter on supervision and inspection is included in the Urban and Rural Planning Law to strengthen supervisory and inspection measures as well as supervision by the people's congress, the general public and executive sectors on urban-rural planning so that the mechanism of supervision and management of urban-rural planning will be legislatively underpinned and the guidance and regulation of urban-rural planning in urban-rural construction will be further boosted.

1. Administrative supervision in urban-rural planning

The stipulations of the Urban and Rural Planning Law on urban-rural planning with regard to administrative supervision are as follows:

(1) Supervision and inspection of people's governments above county level and their competent urban-rural planning departments on lower-level governments and their competent urban-rural planning departments in their execution of the formulation, approval, implementation and modification of urban-rural planning. For instance, the urban-rural planning mechanism of supervisors established jointly by the Ministry of Construction, Sichuan, Guizhou and other provinces (or cities) effectively involves supervisors being sent by the people's government of a higher level and its competent urban-rural planning department to lower-level people's governments and their competent urban-rural planning departments to have an overall supervision on the formulation, approval, implementation and management of urban-rural planning.

(2) Supervision and inspection on the implementation of urban-rural planning by competent urban-rural planning departments under local people's governments above county level, namely the relative person of management commonly referred to.

2. Supervision of people's congress on urban-rural planning

Article 52 of the Urban and Rural Planning Law stipulates that a local people's government shall report the implementation situation of urban-rural planning to the standing committee of the people's congress at the same level or the people's congress of the township or town, and shall be subject to the latter's supervision.

3. Supervision of the public on urban-rural planning

It is stipulated in the Urban and Rural Planning Law that supervision, inspection and disposal of urban-rural planning shall be disclosed to the general public pursuant to the law for people to consult and supervise.

Source of data: Office of Economic Law of the Commission of Legislative Affairs of the NPC Standing Committee, Law Department of Agro-Environmental Protection of the Legislative Affairs Office of the State Council, Urban and Rural Planning Department of the Ministry of Housing and Urban-rural Development, *Interpretation on the Urban and Rural Planning Law of the People's Republic of China*, edited by the Policy and Law Department and published by Intellectual Property Press (2008)

III. Drafting, Modification and Implementation of Urban-rural Planning

The operating system of urban-rural planning consists of the compilation, modification and implementation of planning (often referred to as development planning and development controlling in many other countries).

1. Drafting

Despite variations in the formulating mechanism used in different countries, two parameters are universally recognized: urban-rural development planning and controlling. Urban-rural development planning, which constitutes the medium- and long-term objective in planning urban development as well as the countermeasure for land use, traffic control, allocation of facilities and environmental protection, aims to provide a guiding framework for the planning of development control of all areas in cities. As the legal basis on which the planning formulated is implemented, the planning of development control shall be compiled in accordance with relevant planning laws in terms of both contents and procedures, which is why it is otherwise referred to as statutory planning.

In China, urban-rural development planning is comparable to comprehensive urban planning (including district planning of large and medium-sized cities) and comprehensive planning of towns, townships and villages; and planning of development control is tantamount to regulatory planning. The regional urban system planning of all levels provides the basis for comprehensive urban planning, while site detailed planning only serves as the foundation for development control in given cases (e.g. the key areas whose construction plan has been put into practice).

2. Modification

To guarantee that urban-rural planning is carried out scientifically and seriously and to bring it under full supervision in order to improve the sustainable development of urban-rural construction, the Urban and Rural Planning Law includes an extra chapter on the modification of urban-rural planning so that a strictly-controlled mechanism for averting any attempt to change statutory planning will be legislatively defined and established.

(1) Modification of provincial urban system planning, overall city planning and overall town planning

Article 47 of the Urban and Rural Planning Law stipulates that only the authority responsible for the formulation of urban-rural planning shall be entitled to modify provincial urban system planning, overall city planning and overall town planning within its power limits and in accordance with prescribed procedures in any of the following cases:

A. Changes in urban-rural planning established by the people's government at a higher level require modification of the planning;

B. Adjustment of administrative divisions requires modification of the planning;

C. A significant construction project approved by the State Council requires modification of the planning;

D. Modification is necessary upon evaluation. Article 46 says that the organ establishing a provincial urban system planning, overall city planning or overall town planning shall organize related departments and experts to evaluate the implementation of the planning on a regular basis and collect public opinion by argumentation, hearing or other ways. The organ shall submit an evaluation report attached with the collected opinions to the standing committee of the people's congress at the same level, the people's congress of the town and the organ examining and approving the planning;

E. Other circumstances under which modification is necessary as deemed by the organ examining and approving urban-rural planning.

Before modifying the provincial urban planning system and the overall planning of cities and towns, the organ establishing it shall summarize the implementation of the planning and report the situation to the organ responsible for examining and approving the planning. If the modification involves the mandatory content of the city or town overall planning, the organ establishing it shall submit a special report to the organ that examines and approves the planning, and shall gear up for the modification plan after obtaining the consent of the organ examining and approving the planning. The modified provincial urban system planning, overall city planning or overall town planning shall be filed for approval in accordance with the examining and approving procedures.

(2) Modification of immediate construction planning

Regulatory detailed planning constitutes not only the immediate legal basis for a city or town to exercise planning administration, but also the legal precondition for the leasing of the right to use state-owned land as well as the development and construction relevant to it (see Chapter 5 for more about land used for construction in China). In this light, it directly determines the market value of land as well as the immediate interests of stakeholders. No unit or person, therefore, shall be entitled to any unauthorized modification of the regulatory planning.

Modification of regulatory detailed planning must be conducted in strict conformity with legal procedure. According to Article 48 of the Urban and Rural Planning Law, to modify regulatory planning, the organ establishing it shall register the necessity of the modification, take counsel with interested persons within the planning area, submit a special report to the organ examining and approving it, and stand ready for the modification plan after obtaining the consent of the organ examining and approving the planning. The modified regulatory detailed planning shall be filed for approval in accordance with the examining and approving procedures as prescribed in Articles 19 and 20 of this law. If the modification involves the mandatory content of the city or overall town planning, the overall planning shall be modified first.

3. Implementation

The Urban and Rural Planning Law stipulates that the system of 'one proposal and two permits' (a written proposal of location, a construction land-use permit and a planning permit on construction project) shall be adopted in China's urban planning administration and that the system of planning permission for rural construction shall be exercised in China's rural planning administration. The legally stipulated written proposal of location, the construction land use permit, the planning permit on the construction project and the planning permit for rural construction have combined to constitute the primary means and modes in the implementation and administration of China's urban-rural planning, of which the issuing of the written proposal of location pertains to administrative examination and approval while the construction land-use permit, the planning permit on construction project and the planning permit for rural construction belongs to administrative licensing.

(1) Administration of location planning for construction projects

The administration of location planning for construction projects guarantees the competent administrative department responsible for urban-rural planning to first determine or select the locations of construction projects in compliance with the urban-rural planning and related laws and regulations so that all construction shall be arranged in agreement with the urban-rural planning and then issue the written proposals of locations after checking and verification.

The Urban and Rural Planning Law clearly defines the applicable range of the written proposals of location. Article 36 of the law stipulates: "As for a construction project that is subject to the approval or verification of the related department as required by state provisions, if the right to use state-owned land is appropriated, the construction entity shall, before filing the project with the related department for approval, apply to the competent department of urban and rural planning to issue a written proposal of location."

(2) Administration of construction land-use planning

The administration of planning for construction land enables the competent administrative department responsible for urban-rural planning, in conformity with the legal norms of urban-rural planning and the planning established according to law, to determine the site, location and range of the land for construction, examine and verify the gross areas of the construction projects, furnish design conditions for land use and issue construction land-use permits.

As for now, the construction entities in China have two main ways to acquire the right to use state-owned land: appropriation and leasing (see Special Column 2-4). The land for construction acquired through different means involves different planning management.

Special Column 2-4 Acquisition of the right to use land for construction[8]

At present, construction entities in China have two main ways to acquire the right to use state-owned land: appropriation and leasing.

Appropriating the right to use state-owned land means that land users shall be consigned with the land after they have paid compensation, resettlement allowance and other expenses with the approval of the people's government at or above county level. Appropriated land falls into four general categories: land used by state organs and the army, land for common facilities and public welfare establishments, land for energy development, transportation, hydraulic engineering and other infrastructure supported by the state, and land for other uses stipulated by laws and administrative regulations.

Leasing of the right to use state-owned land means that the state consigns the right to use state-owned land within a term of years to the land users who pay to the state leasing fees for the right to use the land. Leasing of the right to the use of state-owned land may be materialized by means of tender invitation, auction, quotation or agreement. In conformity with current laws and regulations, land for commerce, tourism, entertainment industries, commercial housing and all kinds of uses of land for business purposes shall have to be obtained through tender invitation, auction or price-listing.

A. Application for construction land-use permit in case of appropriation

If the right to the use of state-owned land for a construction project within a city or town planning area is appropriated, upon the approval or verification of the related department, or archiving of the project, the construction entity shall apply to the competent department of urban and rural planning under the people's government of the city or town for permitting land use for construction. The department shall issue a construction land-use permit after checking and verifying the location and area of the land used for construction as well as the scope of areas where construction is permitted in accordance with detailed regulatory planning.

The construction entity may only apply to the competent department of land under the local people's government at or above county level for land

---
[8] See Chapter 5 for more about China's land system

use after obtaining the land-use permit. The competent department of land may appropriate land to it upon the approval of the people's government at or above county level.

B. Application for planning permit on construction project in case of assignment

If the right to use state-owned land within a city or town planning area is leased, the competent department of urban and rural planning under the people's government of the city or county shall, before leasing, raise planning requirements such as the location of the land to be leased, the nature of its use and development intensity as a component of the leasing contract for the right to use state-owned land on the basis of detailed regulatory planning.

If the right to use state-owned land for a construction project is obtained through leasing, the construction entity shall, after concluding the leasing contract for the right to use state-owned land, obtain the land-use permit from the competent department of urban and rural planning of the people's government of the city or county upon the strength of the approval, or verification or archive-filing documents of the project as well as the leasing contract for the right to use state-owned land.

(3) Management of construction engineering planning

The management of construction engineering planning authorizes the competent administrative department responsible for urban-rural planning to organize, regulate, guide and coordinate all kinds of construction projects so as to have them included in the system of urban-rural planning before issuing planning permits for rural construction in accordance with the urban-rural planning legally established as well as related legal and technical norms.

To build any structure, fixture, road, pipeline or other engineering project within a city or town planning area, the construction entity or individual shall apply to the competent department of urban and rural planning under the people's government of the city or county or the town people's government specified by the people's government of the province, autonomous region or municipality directly under the central government for a construction project planning permit.

(4) Management of rural construction planning

To build facilities needed by township and village enterprises, village public utilities or public welfare establishments within a township or village planning area, the construction entity or individual shall file an application with the people's government of the township or town, which shall submit the application to the competent department of urban and rural planning of the people's government of the city or county for issuing a planning permit for rural construction.

When building premises needed by township and village enterprises, rural common facilities or public welfare establishments within a township or village planning area, no farm land may be used. Where it is really necessary to use farm land, the competent department of urban and rural planning under the people's government of the city or county may issue a planning permit for rural construction after the construction entity or individual reckons with the examining and approving formalities for changing the purpose of farm land in accordance with the relevant provisions of the Land Administration Law of the PRC.

The construction entity or individual may not handle the examining and approving formalities for land use until they obtain the planning permit for rural construction.

Chapter 3

Industrial Distribution in Cities

I. Dominant Functions of Cities and their Industrial Layout

The function of cities refers to the part they play in national or regional economic development.[9] With the growth of cities from small towns with a single function into metropolises with multi-faceted roles, their dominant functions have been undergoing dynamic change. The industrial layout of cities is the spatial manifestation of their functions[10] and the evolution of the leading functions of cities in China constitutes the root cause for the adjustment of urban industrial layout.

1. Changes in the Dominant Function of Cities

(1) Production as the dominant function of cities prior to reform and opening up

China has enjoyed thousands of years' agricultural civilization. At the founding of the PRC, the country was still in the preindustrial era when its cities with an indistinctive function of production were in large part exchange centers for commodities that offered fragmentary services such as political leadership, administrative jurisdiction by military means, with their consumer attributes far outweighing their production properties. In 1952, the nation's total industrial output accounted for only 17.6% of gross domestic product (GDP). Cities relied on rural areas for farm products, while they were incapable of providing adequate and decent manufactured goods for both themselves and the countryside. Therefore, the promotion of production and the transformation of consumer cities into cities also

---

[9] Yu Hongjun & Ning Yuemin. *Outline of Urban Geography* [M]. Hefei: Anhui Science and Technology Press, 1983
[10] Chu Tianjiao. *Revelations from the Evolution of the CBD in Urban Transformation in Singapore* [J]. *Modern Urban Research*, 2011,(10)

featuring production became a pressing need for consolidating the newly-established people's regime, improving the living standard of the public and enabling China to survive and then prosper among world nations in the long run. When the first Five-year Plan was under way, therefore, China started to set about developing urbanization with a focus on the construction of key projects empowered with industrialization.

From the 1950s to the 1970s, under the guidance of the urban development strategy to slow down the expansion of big cities and boost the growth of small and medium-sized cities, urbanization in China progressed in a gradual and fluctuating way. With the driving of key projects, a number of new cities were constructed while old cities were developed into regional industrial production centers. The capital of the country and all provincial capitals prospered into production centers with degrees of comprehensiveness and specialization, but the majority of county towns also fared well and began to develop the so-called 'five types of small industries'.[11] As a result, production-based urban systems of different levels took shape across the country. The share of secondary industrial output in GDP rose steadily to 48.5% by 1980. However, due to an excessive emphasis on the manufacturing function of cities, coupled with an exorbitant stress on the roles of cities as industrial bases, the development of heavy industry was over-emphasized while light industry and the service sector trailed behind with the result that urban infrastructure, service facilities and housing supply became extremely deficient.[12] During this period, the growth in agricultural labor productivity and the ability to supply agricultural products clearly lagged behind the pace of industrial

---

[11] 'Five types of small industries' is the general reference to small local or regional factories and mines. During the 1960s, it referred to small workshops, small coal mines, small power stations, small fertilizer plants and small machinery works. Later on, small cement plants and other small enterprises were further included. In 1970 when the fourth Five-year Plan was carried out, the central government appealed to all provinces and autonomous regions to speed up the development of five types of small industries and decided that eight billion yuan would be appropriated from the state revenue as a special fund for the development of five types of small local industries. The growth of small industries that helped change the structure of China's industrial economy increased the proportion of small and medium-sized industrial entities in industrial enterprises and made it possible for small and medium-sized enterprises to rationally undertake responsibilities in line with the principle of specialization and cooperation. Small and medium-sized enterprises could complement or supplement large enterprises and, what is more, they could make better use of local resources. In summary, the development of small enterprises significantly enhanced the strength of the local economy and greatly improved the economic situation of individual counties that would change their previous practices from sole reliance on agriculture to an adequate amount of industry with agricultural production as the focus, and in the meantime moderately increase the income of non-agricultural employers. On the other hand, however, the booming development of five types of small industries had its flaws and would bring about negative consequences

[12] Chu Tianjiao. *General Mechanism of Regional Expansion in Urbanization* [J]. *Economic Geography*, 1998, (6)

development in cities. Moreover, the household registration system and other measures that imposed restrictions on the transfer of surplus labor forces in rural areas to non-agricultural sectors in cities made urbanization fall behind industrialization. This period, therefore, is also referred to as an era of 'industrialization without urbanization'. From 1949-1980, the number of cities in China increased from 136 to only 193, with an average annual growth rate of 1.84, while the proportion of the non-agricultural population to the total population in urban areas grew respectively from 9.1% and 10.6% to 13.7% and 19.4%.[13]

(2) Focus on coordination between production and service after reform and opening up

Beginning from the mid-1980s, China started to focus on the driving role of big cities in developing regional economies. It also lent support to the development of enterprises under all forms of ownership, small and medium-sized enterprises and township enterprises in rural areas along with its efforts to develop small cities and towns so as to promote the interaction between cities and regional economies from the bottom up. The vigorous expansion of small cities and towns made it possible for the massive surplus rural workforces to easily transfer to non-agricultural sectors and thus helped alleviate the pressures on the migration of population in medium- and large-sized cities.

The service industry plays a remarkable role in guaranteeing the driving role of medium- and large-sized cities in the growth of a regional economy. Since the 1980s, considerable progress has been made in China's infrastructure construction and service industry, the urban economic structure having thus been adjusted and the economic strength intensified. The rapid development of economies under all forms of ownership and township enterprises helped promote the rapid expansion of moderate-sized cities and small towns, which not only touched off the climax of urban construction between the end of the 1980s and the beginning of the 1990s, but also brought into being a number of agglomerated urban areas in eastern China. The number of cities increased from 193 in 1980 to 668 in 1998, with an average annual growth of 26.39 cities and the ratio of the non-agricultural population to the total population rising, respectively, from 13.7% and 19.4% to 23.97% and 30.4%. The function of the tertiary industry in economic development received greater attention and its development was subsidized, the proportion

---

[13] Zhou Yixing. *Urban Geography* [M]. Beijing: Commercial Press, 1997

of its contribution to GDP having increased from 21.4% in 1980 to 32.9% in 1998. During this period, the percentage of secondary industry only increased from 48.5% to 48.7%, while the proportion of industrial output shrank from 44.2% to 42.1%. Industrial output, however, still outweighed that of tertiary industry and the number of non-agricultural employees did not surpass those living and working in rural areas until 1997, which indicates that China at the time was still at the stage of development with industrialization as the driving force.[14]

As it came to the 1990s, the function of cities in China started to shift from a focus on production to the services sector.[15] Generally, if the number of employees in the tertiary industry is more than half of total employment, it is an indicator that the country has entered a post-industrial society where manufacturing industry has given way to the service-oriented economy. Pilot projects were under way in the late 1980s in China. Starting from the 1990s, paid transfer or assignment of land and the reform of state-owned enterprises (SOEs) and the housing system in cities were launched in a comprehensive way, which triggered the relocation of urban industries,[16] the vast stretches of industrial land in downtown areas having thus been transformed into land for tertiary industry. The rapid progress of real estate, finance, insurance, transportation, post and telecommunications and other sectors demonstrated a gradual strengthening of the leading role of tertiary industry. With the adjustment of industrial and land-use structures as well as rising public demand for promoting the quality of their life, city governments set about intensifying environmental renovation, upgrading infrastructure and service facilities, constructing green space and improving living conditions in downtown areas, thereby starting to transform production-centered cities into service-oriented and lifestyle-based metropolises such as in Beijing, Shanghai, Guangzhou and Shenzhen. In these cities, the functions of both traditional shopping centers and modern business districts became more prominent[17] and well-appointed and environment-friendly residential and recreational centers were built in the outskirts of downtown areas to cater for residents of different income levels.

---

[14] Xu Xueqiang. *Urbanization in China: Theory and Practices* [M]. Beijing: Science Press, 2012
[15] Research group of 'Development Trend of Urban Planning in China' from China Academy of Urban Planning and Design. Development Trend of Urban Planning in China, 1997-1998 [J]. *Urban Planning Forum*. 1998, (4). pages 3-11
[16] Chu Tianjiao. *Dynamic Mechanism of Regional Industrial Division and Cooperation within the Context of Economic Globalization* [J]. Academic Journal of Zhongzhou, 2010, (2)
[17] Chu Tianjiao. *Life Insurance Companies in China: Distribution and Selection of Locations* [J]. World Economic Geography, 2010, (1)

2. Dominant Function and Adjustment of Industrial Layout, with Shanghai as an Example

The industrial distribution in Shanghai before the 1980s was heavily skewed towards the city center. The layout was a legacy of the city's historical development and was a result of the single function of cities that prevailed in the planned economy. As industry in Shanghai took shape during the semi-colonial era before the PRC was founded, a large number of plants and factories were concentrated within the concessions downtown. After the New China was established, Shanghai worked out its guideline of urban construction to build itself into a production-centered city (see Figure 3-1). It is only natural, therefore, that an over-reliance on the established industrial base would result in single function of the city and in the meantime the rational distribution of industry would be overlooked.

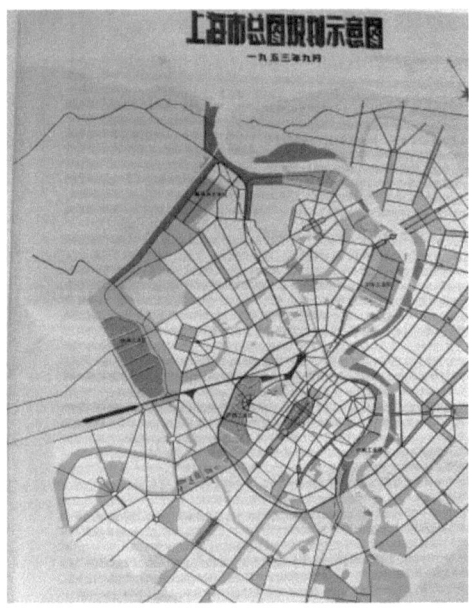

Figure 3-1 Sketch map of the General Planning of Shanghai worked out in September 1953 with the guidance of A. S. Mukhin, an expert from the former Soviet Union

In the 1950s, Shanghai finished building eight industrial parks in Pengpu, Beixinjing and other suburban areas, along with seven industrial satellite towns beyond the city suburbs, such as Minhang, Wujing and Anting (see Figure 3-2). As the inner city was constantly expanding, however, the problem with the industrial concentration in the downtown area had still not been thoroughly addressed by the 1980s. According to statistics, the number of industrial enterprises, the employed population and gross industrial output within the inner city and covering an area of 216 square kilometers accounted for, respectively, 47%, 60% and 66% of the city's entire industry by the end of 1987. Industrial density was even higher in the 10 administrative districts in the downtown area, with their numbers making up 43.8% of the city's total by 1990. The high industrial density in downtown areas gave rise to a shortage of land for industrial enterprises, aggravated urban traffic pressure, caused heavy pollution and confronted urban development with a growing 'spatial crisis'. As a heavy user of urban land, industry's booming progress held up the development of the tertiary industry and impacted the performance of the city's comprehensive role.

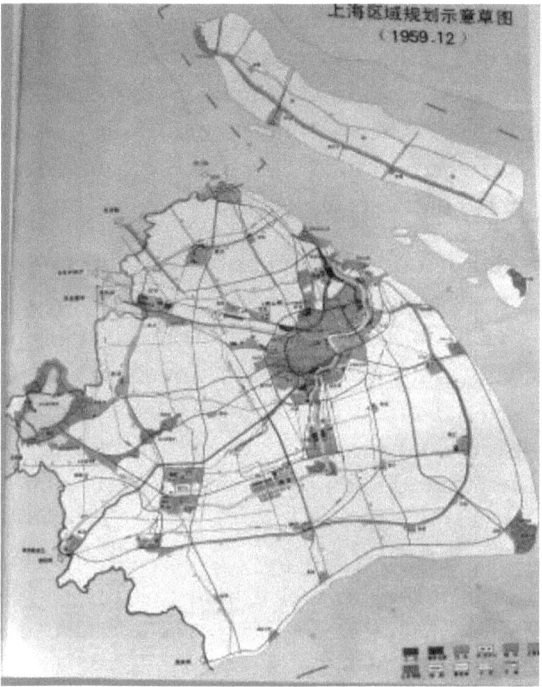

Figure 3-2 Draft of the regional planning of Shanghai worked out in 1959

In the reorientation of its function after the 1990s, Shanghai defined its strategic development goals to establish the city as an international economic, financial, commercial and shipping center and to restructure its industry. Conforming to the goal of urban development, Shanghai followed a policy of 'simultaneous promotion of secondary and tertiary industries' in industrial development throughout the 1990s with priority given to tertiary industry, while adjusting secondary industry and developing primary industry, thereby bringing about a pattern of economic development that was largely driven by secondary industry joining forces with tertiary industry. The exercise of industrial restructuring throughout the period helped increase the share of tertiary industry in GDP from 31.9% in 1990 to 50.6% in 2000; the proportion of secondary industry in GDP dropped from 61.7% to 47.5% over the same period, while the percentage of primary industry fell from 3.8% to 1.8%.

As the distribution of industry was manifested in the spatial projection of its industrial structure, Shanghai's industrial layout, which had previously been oriented toward the development of an urban industrial structure, had to be reshaped so that its spatial distribution of industry came into line with its global urban development planning: finance, trade, commerce and other service sectors were given supremacy in the city center, while a large number of traditional industrial enterprises that were densely distributed in the downtown area were readjusted and relocated. Industrial parks and bases mainly built on pillar and new technology industries were developed in the suburbs and modern ecological and protected urban agriculture businesses were promoted in the outskirts of the city.

By way of restructuring the industrial layout in the 1990s, there emerged a framework of industrial distribution pertaining to a metropolis like Shanghai in which tertiary industry was highlighted in the downtown area and secondary industry assumed a dominant role in the suburbs. Specifically, the central urban area (around 600 square kilometers within the outer ring) was mainly devoted to tertiary industry while secondary and primary industries were developed in the suburbs (approximately 5,700 square kilometers beyond the outer ring). Industrial distribution assumed a pattern in which the tertiary industry, along with some textiles and other light industries, formed the downtown industrial circle while the suburban industrial circle took shape in the outskirts where machinery, electronics, automotive, textiles, emerging heavy chemical industries and allied businesses were prioritized; the basic raw materials industry was developed in the urban fringes and urban agriculture featuring ecology, recreation and breeding was well promoted. Through industrial restructuring, Pudong and other suburban districts or counties turned into important supporting and sustaining areas for Shanghai's industrial development by 2000. By this time, the number of industrial enterprises, employed population and gross industrial output in this area all exceeded 70% of the city's total.

II. Construction of Development Zones: a New Industrial Space

Development zones are important spatial carriers of China's urbanization drive, and key regions that motivate the spatial restructuring of urban industry in China. To have an insight into the evolution of China's urban industrial layout, we have to be well acquainted with the construction of its development zones. As is well known, China's urban population began to burgeon after 1978. And it was the construction of development zones that provided the spatial vehicle and industrial conditions for the expansion of the urban population; if we had simply relied on the natural growth of urban areas, there would not have been adequate room to accommodate an annual increase of around 10 million urban residents. During the renovation of many large and super-large cities and the refurbishment of a great many old urban industrial bases, the policy goal of the 'retreat of secondary industry and advance of tertiary industry' was made possible because the construction of development zones offered maneuvering space for industrial restructuring and emerging industries.

1. History of Development Zones

The genesis of development zones is known to be city-based. They are particular places where preferential policies and special management systems are exercised by the Chinese government as one of the strategic choices in the face of economic globalization and the global revolution in economic technologies. Since the implementation of reform and opening up, China has been exploring its own development path that leads to modern industrialization with Chinese characteristics. It has endeavored to construct development zones that focus on establishing parks of various descriptions, whereupon those parks have become regions of most agglomerated modernized industries that enjoy the fastest economic development, largest foreign investment and the most advanced technologies. The agglomerated modern industrial parks armed with the most advanced technologies function as important platforms and they are flag bearers for China's industrialization, urbanization and internationalization. They have long been the leading growth poles in regional economic development and they have won the stamp of approval of the Party Central Committee and the State Council and commanded the attention of countries worldwide, especially developing ones. By the end of 2006, China had a total of 11,568 state- and province-level development zones with a planning area of 7,629 square kilometers. They were largely distributed in coastal regions or along rivers (the Yangtze in particular), railways (notably the Longhai Railway) and borders or in inland capitals of provinces, autonomous regions, prefectures as well as in central cities (see Figure 3-3). The construction of development zones in China occurred in three stages, as follows.

Figure 3-3 Distribution of state-level economic and technological development zones and high-tech industrial development zones

(1) Exploratory stage (1984-1991)

China's reform and opening up started with the construction of development zones. This stage witnessed the inauguration of state-level economic and technological development zones (ETDZs) and high-tech industrial development zones.[18]

A. Construction of state-level ETDZs

In 1984, the party and the government made a decision to open Dalian, Tianjin, Guangzhou and 11 other port cities to the outside world. It also approved the construction of 11 ETDZs in Dalian, Qinhuangdao, Ningbo, Qingdao, Yantai, Zhanjiang, Guangzhou, Tianjin, Nantong, Lianyungang and Fuzhou so that China could bring in advanced and much-needed technologies from abroad, establish Sino-foreign joint or cooperative ventures, exclusively foreign-owned enterprises and Sino-foreign cooperative research institutes, develop joint production and cooperative research design projects, develop new techniques and high-end products, increase export earnings, supply interior regions with new materials and key components, and disseminate new technologies and techniques along with scientific managerial expertise and practices.[19] In 1986, the State Council approved the construction of two more ETDZs at Hongqiao

---

[18] Gu Chaolin & Wang Hesheng. *Construction and Growth of Development Zones in China* [A]. Edited by Niu Fengrui, Pan Jiahua & Liu Zhiyan. *Development of Cities in China within Three Decades* [C]. Beijing: Social Sciences Academic Press, 2009

[19] *Circular of the State Council on Forwarding the Summary of the Forum of Some Coastal Cities.* May 4, 1984

and Minhang in Shanghai. All these zones have since become the most dynamic and attractive regions to investors and have played pivotal roles in driving China's industrialization, urbanization and construction of a well-off society in a comprehensive way.

B. Construction of state-level high-tech industrial development zones

In 1988, the government, in order to boost technological innovation and commercialization of research findings, approved the establishment of state-level high-tech industrial development zones, the first one being Zhongguancun Science and Technology Park in Beijing. That same year, Caohejing Hi-Tech Park was constructed, based on the Instrumentation and Electronics Industrial Zone, Microelectronics Industrial Zone and Bioengineering Base located in Shanghai.

(2) Stage of booming development (1992-1996)

After two years' improvement and rectification from 1989 to 1990,[20] China's economy moved into a phase of revival and rapid progress in 1991 when the construction of development zones started to gather pace while various development areas advanced rapidly and bonded areas, tourist resorts and other new types of development zone were established.

During this period, development zone construction began to push westward along the great rivers and a nationwide 'development zone spree' was under way when all provinces and cities across the country spared no effort in constructing their own development zones. By the end of 1994, a total of some 700 state-, province- and city-level development zones had been established, including 32 state-level economic and technological zones, 52 national high-tech industrial parks, 13 national bonded areas, 11 national tourist resorts and the Suzhou-Singapore Industrial Park. Among these development zones, the bonded areas and 91.7% of national tourist resorts were located in eastern coastal regions, while the locations of other types and levels of development zones were quite widely dispersed.

Construction of development zones at this stage had three main features. First, the scale and quality of foreign investments were upgraded.

---

[20] With the rapid progress in reforming the economic system from 1985 to 1988, the overheated development of China's economy persisted while inflation worsened. From 1989 to 1990, China positively adjusted its economic structure by cutting down the total demand of society and tightening control over expenditure and credit and in the long run managed to bring inflation under control, its industrial restructuring having thus been launched

Multinational corporations replaced small and medium-sized enterprises to become major investors. They invested in projects with a reasonably high technical content and funded a number of research and development centers,[21] foreign investment in China having then grown substantially in scale. Motorola, for instance, invested 1.1 billion US dollars in Tianjin Development Zone in 1992 to become the leading foreign-owned enterprise in China at the time. Second, the zones made high profile achievements in terms of economic strength, value of industrial output, tax revenue and economic benefit. In 1996, the industrial output of the 14 economic and technological development zones in the coastal regions increased by 858% compared with that in 1991. Third, the share of economic output of development zones in the cities in which they were located increased. In 1996, the industrial output of Guangzhou Development Zone accounted for 11.2% of the city's total, while that of Tianjin Development Area took up 18% of the city's total, which indicates that development zones had already become sizable growth poles in the urban economy.[22]

(3) Stage of sustained progression (1997-date)

The outbreak of the Asian financial crisis in 1997 gave rise to a sharp downturn in foreign investment in China's development zones. The crisis highlighted the huge risks involved in developing an export-oriented economy and triggered a phase of adjustment, transformation and upgrading in the construction of development zones. In this period, the guideline for the construction of development zones was shifted from a dependence on attracting foreign capital to one that stressed the need to introduce both domestic and overseas capital, cultivating embeddedness of industries and promoting the transformation and upgrading of industrial structure. In the meantime, differences between development zones were exposed in terms of economic performance and waste of land resources. In 2004, the government reorganized all development zones and optimized their structure by canceling or merging many zones that were inferior in economic performance. By 2007, 1,568 state- and province-level development zones had passed national approval after rectification and reorganization, of which 223 were state level (see Table 3-1). Those zones that passed approval were of great importance to the nation's economy in attracting investment, generating imports and exports, and overall industrial development (see

---

[21] Chu Tianjiao & Song Tao. *Spatial Patterns and Contributing Factors for R&D Investments of Multinational Corporations in Developing Countries* [J]. Economic Geography, 2006, (1)
[22] Wang Fengyu & Zhu Xiaojuan. *China Development Zones Development Review and Strategic Thinking* [J]. Yunnan Geographic Environment Research, 2006, (4), page 96

Table 3-2). To date, national high-tech industrial development zones have evolved into important bases of China's modern manufacturing industry and high-tech industrialization.

Table 3-1 Types and numbers of development zones in China (2007)

Levels	Types	Number	Remarks
State-level development zones	Total	223	
	ETDZs	54	Including Suzhou Industrial Park, Jinqiao Export Processing Zone (Shanghai), Ningbo ETDZ, Haichang Taiwanese Investment Zone (Xiamen) and Yangpu Economic Development Zone (Hainan) that enjoy preferential policies for state-level ETDZs
	High-tech industrial development zones	54	
	Export processing zones	57	
	Bonded areas	16	
	Bonded logistic parks	6	
	Taiwanese investment zones	4	
	Cross-Strait sci-tech industrial parks	2	
	Border economic cooperation zones	14	
	Border trade districts	2	
	National resort districts	12	
	Cross-border industrial zones	1	Zhuhai-Macau Cross-border Industrial District is China's only state-level development zone across two administrative regions
	Finance and trade zones	1	Lujiazui Finance and Trade Zone in Pudong, Shanghai, is the country's only state-level development zone, mainly engaged in finance and trade

Province-level Development Zones	Total	1,345	
	Economic development zones	810	
	Industrial parks	535	Includes 64 high-tech industrial parks
Total		1,568	

Source: National Development and Reform Commission (NDRC)

Table 3-2 Major economic indicators for state-level development zones for the economic and technological industry (2006)

Indexes	GDP (billion RMB)	Industrial added value (billion RMB)	Tax revenue (billion RMB)	Total export-import volume (billion USD)	Total export volume (billion USD)	Total import volume (billion USD)	Actual foreign investment (billion USD)
Development zones	1,013.690	741.424	157.002	283.096	149.233	133.863	14.712
National total	20,940.7	9,035.1	3,763.6	1,760.7	969.1	791.6	63.0
Percentage of development zones in national total	4.84%	8.21%	4.17%	16.08%	15.40%	16.91%	23.35%

Source: Ministry of Commerce

Moving into the 21st century, China continued to enjoy a steady growth in the construction of development zones. Take state-level development zones. At the end of the 11th Five-year Plan, there were 116 state-level development zones, their economic output having kept on expanding, the growth of their major economic indicators all in excess of the national average and their contribution to the national economy having steadily increased. Over the course of the 11th Five-year Plan, the total output value of state-level development zones increased at an annual rate of 23%, with its share of the national total having increased by 7%, the proportion of their industrial added value standing at 12%, the rate of their gross exports accounting for 16% and the percentage of their gross tax revenue standing at 6%. Compared with the levels at the end of the 10th Five-year Plan, these indicators had grown by 2%, 3%, 0.5% and 1.5% respectively. Moreover, the economic driving capacity of state-level development zones for local regions was strengthened, the gross value of production they generated accounting for more than 13% of the total of the cities in which they were located.

2. Influence of Development Zones on Remodeling Urban Industrial Space

For China, the original purposes of establishing development zones were to attract foreign capital and develop the high-tech and export processing industries. With the passage of time, however, development zones achieved more than this, becoming robust economic growth poles of local cities, the main platform for an export-oriented economy, the core area of innovation systems and the forefront of reform and opening up. In addition, they developed into the major driving force and key vehicle for urbanization.[23] Development zones were not only important venues where newly arrived peasants were expected to change their career and way of life, but the most significant regions that would spearhead the modernization of urban areas. Construction of development zones has enabled many cities to pool their massive industries and populations within a limited time period, and they have also played a crucial role in promoting local cities' industrial upgrading, optimization of urban spatial organization, improvement and elevation of urban functions, renewal and regeneration of urban infrastructure, and construction of new urban districts. Development zones, therefore, can be seen as important carriers or vehicles of China's urbanization.

The spatial relationship between China's development zones and the local cities has witnessed two stages of evolution.

(1) Development zones' 'isolated island' stage (1984-mid-1990s)

To moderate the highly probable impact and interference imposed by foreign-funded enterprises on China's economic system, development zones were established at the start in locations a short distance from urban areas. In fact, they were virtually 'isolated islands', spatially set apart from the local cities by roads, rivers and other geographic boundaries. At this stage, all development zones in China bore a resemblance to export processing zones in foreign countries in terms of functions. By taking advantage of China's inexpensive workforce and preferential policies, foreign-funded enterprises came to invest and establish operations in development zones, their scale of investment being relatively small and their technical merits inadequate. In general, the enterprises were remote from the economy of local cities because their raw materials and markets were both absent locally, which is why development zones established at that stage are now known as 'isolated islands'.

---

[23] Zheng Guo. *Growth of Development Zones and Reconstruction of Urban Space in China: Implications and History* [J]. Modern Urban Research, 2011, (5), pages 20-24

(2) Development zones merging with cities stage (mid-1990s-)

Beginning from the mid-1990s, development zones started to proliferate both in number and in scale. Almost all cities rushed to plan and construct their own development zones. After 1998, when the guideline for constructing development zones was shifted from a previous reliance on inviting foreign capital to an emphasis on attracting both domestic and overseas capital while the focus of foreign-funded enterprises shifted from exports to both exports and the domestic market, the economic tie between individual enterprises and that between enterprises and local cities within development zones was bolstered when their growth pole effect started to come into play and their driving role in urban economic development was appreciably strengthened. In the meantime, as the expansion of urban infrastructure construction enabled urban areas to further extend and the overall layout of cities started to move from a monocentric to polycentric pattern, development zones and industrial districts of cities became increasingly connected to urban areas.

Thanks to its strong starting point, manufacturing industry in development zones generally represented the development trend of urban areas. At this stage, development zones took a lead in the spatial evolution of manufacturing industry in cities and had a clear and far-reaching effect on the industrial, residential and social space as well as social forms in urban areas. To begin with, the construction of development zones helped accelerate restructuring of urban manufacturing space and facilitated a fresh proliferation and concentration in the spatial structure of urban manufacturing industry, development zones having turned into a place where competitive urban manufacturing industries congregated. Second, the advance of development zones helped drive the suburbanization of the urban population and socio-spatial differentiation. At this stage, upscale communities dominated by affluent groups were attracted to development zones. Finally, due to the comparatively large scale of China's development zones and as a result of the expansion of land for industry that characterized China's urbanization at the time, development zone progress largely held sway over the reconstruction of the urban spatial pattern.

With the aggregation of industries, populations and diverse parameters of production along with the constant improvement in structure and function, development zones now increasingly border on urbanized areas in terms of density of population, level of facility and type of function. The visible and invisible 'boundaries' between development zones and other urban areas are breaking down and, in the long run, they will merge through unceasing amalgamation.

III. Development of New Urban Districts: Reconstruction of Industrial Space

During China's rapid urbanization, construction of new urban districts has become a priority and an effective measure to ease the pressure on population and industry in the downtown area and optimize the regional space of metropolises. At the beginning of the 21st century, when planning and construction of new urban districts was under way in many big cities in China, the formation of a more rational pattern of industrial division between new and old urban districts helped improve the industrial space.

1. Construction of New Urban Districts in China: Background

The history of new urban districts in China can be traced back to the building of satellite towns in the 1950s. Since these satellite towns were relatively small and contained few industrial sectors and ancillary facilities, they could play only a very limited role in addressing problems relating to the urban population and industry because they were of little attraction to residents.

Within the context of economic globalization and deepening of reform and opening up at the end of the 20th century, China's economy, society and urbanization entered a rapid and sustained phase of development. However, the over-density of the population and economic and social activities in metropolises gave rise to huge pressure on normal urban operation. Without reform of the prevailing urban structure, the further development of big cities would be constrained. In this regard, it became a key consideration for metropolitan governments to further expand urban development space, optimize urban structure, relieve pressure on population growth in old urban districts and boost the comprehensive competitiveness of their cities. This being the case, a growing number of big cities began to take the initiative to construct new urban districts in order to enlarge urban space. The purpose was to rationalize the layout and distribution of industries and populations. This meant relocating the population in downtown areas and moderating the pressure on the population and aggregated industries in city centers, while at the same time focusing on the urbanization of suburbs so as to arrest the probable flooding of the population into downtown areas.

Scholar Li Guiwen et al have reviewed the deep-seated factors explaining the rapid development of new urban districts in China since 2000.[24]

First, urban economic development has triggered demand for an expansion of urban space. Since the implementation of reform and opening up, urban areas have been spearheading the development of China's economy and this pattern of growth enables resource elements and populations to congregate in urban areas. Congregation and diffusion constitute two major manifestations in the development of cities. In highly developed metropolises, such as Beijing, Shanghai and Guangzhou, urban areas are no longer in a position to accommodate excessive populations and industries due to limited resources and space and therefore urban functions begin to extend outward and new urban districts have taken shape in the process of expansion and proliferation.

Second, the accelerated reform of land systems has changed the spatial pattern of urban industries. Since the reform and opening up was launched, the exercise of the system of paid use of land, coupled with the growth of the land market, has helped promote the efficiency of land use. The effect of land prices has made it possible for downtown areas to develop into places where commerce, trade, finance and other high-profit industries congregate, while activities such as industry and storage sectors tend to gravitate toward the suburbs where land is less expensive. These new urban districts in the vicinity of metropolises have become major areas that have facilitated a shift in functions.

Third, the reform of the housing system enables urban residents to choose where they would like to settle down. Since the second half of 1998, all towns and cities across the country have stopped the practice of allocating housing and replaced it with a free market in housing distribution. As house prices increased in central downtown areas, new urban districts have been attracting many residents with newly-built and reasonably-priced homes, thereby bringing about the rapid development of real estate and residential quarters in new urban districts.

Fourth, improvements in traffic and transportation have shortened the temporal and spatial distance between new urban districts and downtown with the accelerated development of rail lines and bus rapid transit. By the end of 2005, 10 cities in China – Beijing, Shanghai, Tianjin, Guangzhou, Changchun, Dalian, Chongqing, Wuhan, Shenzhen and Nanjing – had put

---

[24] Li Guiwen, Zhang Xueyong & Zeng Yu. *Conditions for Construction of New Urban Districts in China – with Beijing, Shanghai and Guangzhou as Examples* [J]. Huazhong Architecture, 2011, (2)

into operation urban rail transit networks. Moreover, networked rail transit in cities that shortens the commuting time between new urban districts and downtown has greatly helped strengthen the links between them and promoted the development of the former.

Unlike those industrial satellite towns established in the 1950s, the new urban districts constructed in China since the beginning of the 21st century have been on a larger scale, and boast more comprehensive functions and greater possibilities of 'balanced self-development'.

2. Optimization of Industrial Space via Development of New Urban Districts

(1) System of new urban districts in Beijing

Beijing is the capital of the PRC, and was among the first cities where satellite towns were built. Since the beginning of the 21st century, construction of new urban districts has been taken as a key initiative to decentralize urban residents and industries. In line with its master urban planning for 2004-2020, Beijing has laid out its urban spatial structure according to the design concept of 'double axis-two belts-multicenter' and thus brought into being 11 new urban districts to form a configuration that is typical of 'central city-new urban districts-towns' (see Figure 3-4). The central city, occupying an area of around 1,085 square kilometers, mainly focuses on political, cultural and economic functions. The new urban districts built on previous satellite towns enjoy relative independence and are responsible for decentralizing the population in the central city, aggregating new industries and shepherding regional development. Of the 11 projected new urban districts, Tongzhou, Shunyi and Yizhuang have been identified as priority development areas with a planned population of 0.7-0.9 million.

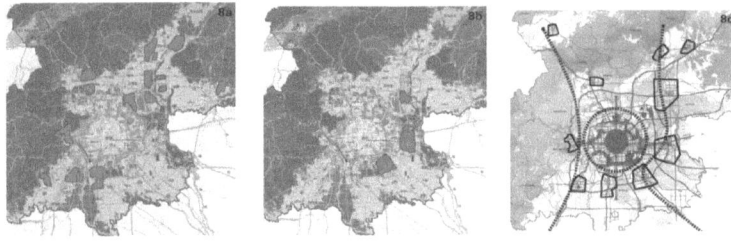

Figure 3-4 Distribution of new urban districts in Beijing

A. Distribution of the 11 new urban districts; B. The three new urban districts as key construction projects; C. Spatial layout of the new urban districts

Source: Beijing Municipal Planning Bureau

(2) Guangzhou: a polycentric and networked city

Prior to the reform and opening up, the development of Guangzhou, the third largest city in China, was primarily centered on its old urban district. Since the reform and opening up was under way, it has built the Guangzhou ETDZ, Nansha ETDZ, Guangzhou High-tech Industrial Development Zone and Guangzhou Science City, all of which had the attributes of early new urban districts. With Mount Baiyun and the Pearl River located within the city border, Guangzhou is fan-shaped, extending all the way to the east and the north. In 2000, the establishment of Panyu and Huadu as districts paved the way for the spatial growth of the built-up areas. In its new development strategy worked out in 2000, the pattern of its urban expansion was defined as a 'point-axis' model that featured radical development, in which a series of new urban districts would be constructed along the axes of extension toward the east and south. To date, the new urban districts that have benefited from all-round development have succeeded in decentralizing industries and population of the city, and have functioned as robust growth poles on the development axes as laid down in the city's strategic planning. Overall, they will apply themselves to promoting the way of urban expansion, accelerating the adjustment of urban spatial structure and boosting the regional comprehensive competitiveness of the city.

In line with the city's master planning outline for 2011-2020, the land for urban-rural construction will total 1,772 square kilometers and the permanent population will reach 18 million by 2020. The urban spatial layout will be polycentric and networked in structure, comprising 'one metropolitan area, two new urban districts and three sub-centers' (see Figure 3-5). The metropolitan area is identified as the major driver of key urban functions with priority on the development of modern commerce and trade, finance and insurance, cultural innovation, medical and health services, business and sci-tech information, headquarters economy and other modern service sectors. The metropolitan area should also feature an optimized layout of regions, high-end urban functions, protection of history and culture, and promotion of land-use efficiency and environmental quality. The two new urban districts are Nansha New Coastal City and Eastern New Landscape City, their primary functions being to improve comprehensiveness and coherence, enhance comprehensive service capacities, facilitate balance and coordination of residential, employment and public service facilities and their synchronous development with industries, and to attract residents and encourage congregation. The three sub-centers, located at Huadu, Conghua and Zengcheng, function as important vehicles of the overall urban-rural development, the role of which is to enhance comprehensive services, decentralize the population and functions within the metropolitan area, and drive the joint development of, and overall integration between, towns and incorporated villages.

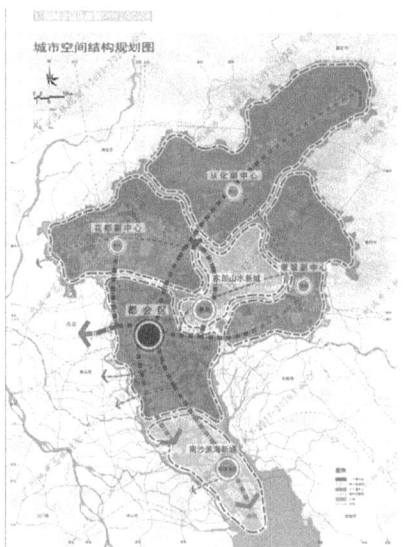

Figure 3-5 Planning map of the urban spatial structure of Guangzhou
Source: Guangzhou Municipal Planning Bureau

(3) New urban district in Ningbo City

The city of Ningbo has long been extending outward, with Sanjiang District as the center. The mode of construction, slow-paced, costly and tending to result in a highly compact old urban district and considerable disorder at the urban-rural fringes, can no longer meet the spatial requirement of the goal to develop Ningbo into an economic center to the south of the Yangtze River Delta. To make up the functional defects of the old urban district and mitigate the problems with the population, housing, traffic, the environment and others, the city government has decided to develop and construct a new urban district.

In line with the city's master urban planning for 2004-2020, Sanjiang District will focus on tertiary industry, production and residential areas, with the moderate development of high-tech or clean industries. The district will centre on the Yuyao, Fenghua and Yong rivers that run through the city. Along these rivers, a cluster of city-level centers of administration, commerce, business, culture and education will be established. The areas within the inner ring will focus on the preservation of the ancient town and the redevelopment of the old district; the district within the middle ring will center on the tertiary industry and residential areas; and the region between the middle ring and the outer ring will be devoted to clean urban industries and residences (see Figure 3-6). A new urban district will be developed and constructed in the east of the old urban district with the purpose of expanding urban development space, relieving pressure on the old district, decentralizing its population and industries, displacing some of the previous functions of the urban center and improving urban functions (see Figure 3-7).

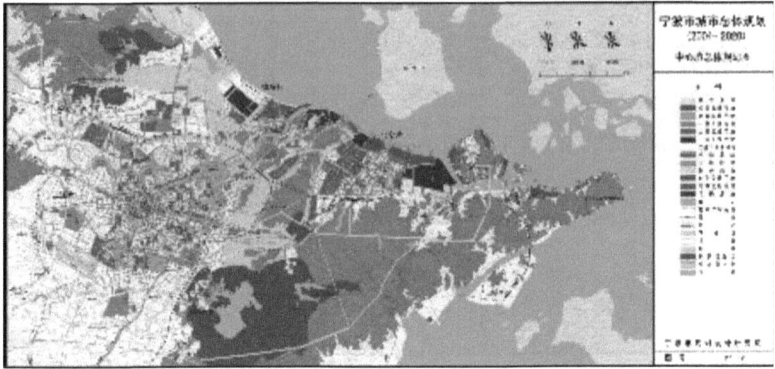

3-6 Master planning of Ningbo City (2004-2020): planning map of the central urban area
Source: Ningbo Municipal Planning Bureau

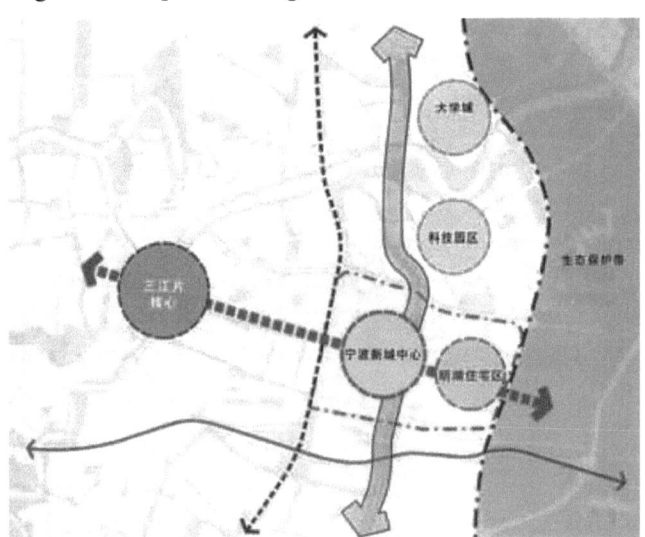

3-7 The new urban district in the east of Ningbo city and its connections with the old town
Source: Ningbo Municipal Planning Bureau

The new urban district is expected to mainly act as a center for administration, science, technology business, information, expositions, eco-leisure and residential homes, and will become the pivot of economic development in Ningbo. In line with this functional orientation, it will turn into a new urban district with a population of around 200,000-300,000, fully functional and relatively independent of the central city.

Chapter 4

Construction of Urban Infrastructure in China

I. History of the Construction of Urban Infrastructure in China

Urban infrastructure is essential for cities to sustain and develop. Urban traffic infrastructure, water supply, drainage, sewage treatment, gas supply, heat supply, power supply, telecommunications, landscaping, environmental health and flood control are closely related to the everyday lives of households. Actually, all economic activity in cities and the life of each and every resident cannot be sustained without them. Large-scale construction and development of urban infrastructure in China started with the implementation of reform and opening up in the 1980s. We may say that China's industrialization and urbanization have significantly promoted the progress of its infrastructural construction to the point that China now stands out as a great and powerful state in terms of infrastructural construction.

Infrastructure encompasses all public utilities or facilities in decent to good condition and they are indispensable for satisfying the needs of residents and the production of all trades and industries in the national economy. As the foundation of other social activities, infrastructural construction plays a crucial role in society at large. Infrastructure can be broken down into various types from different standpoints, the most commonly adopted method being their classification as economic and social infrastructure in terms of their components and supplies. As defined by the World Bank, economic infrastructure includes public utilities, public works and traffic facilities: public utilities consist of electric power, communication, water supply, environmental health, pollution discharge, collection and disposal of solid waste, and pipeline gas; public works refer to highways, railways, dams, irrigation facilities and canals for water drainage; and traffic facilities involve urban transportation, harbors, and air and water transport. Social infrastructure comprises human-generated facilities of culture, education, medicine, insurance and other sectors. This chapter mainly focuses on economic infrastructure.

1. Stage of Inadequacy before Reform and Opening Up

During the two decades or more after the founding of the PRC, investment in infrastructural construction was inadequate, not to mention the spiral of sharp decline that occurred during the Cultural Revolution. The share of infrastructural investment in capital construction investment was about 2% throughout the period. At the beginning of our founding, industry, heavy industry in particular, was given top priority in the nation's economic development plan, while urban development and investment in infrastructure were disregarded to the extent that the construction of infrastructure lagged far behind the development of industry and the urban economy. Inadequate and obsolete infrastructure exacerbated administrative monopoly in the sector, which in turn gave rise to inefficiency and inequity. In the meantime, laws, regulations and institutional policies connected with the planning, construction, operation and management of infrastructure were highly deficient and scant, while enterprises and public institutions engaged in infrastructure were desperately in need of a mechanism and motivation for self-development.[25]

2. Period of Recovery from 1981 to 1990

After the initiation of reform and opening up when governments at all levels and the society at large woke up to the fact that infrastructure played a fundamental role in social and economic development, infrastructural construction started to play a bigger role in economic and social development planning and fixed asset investment nationwide. At the same time, pilot reform was initiated in infrastructural investment, construction and the managerial system. During the decade, the aggregate investment in infrastructure reached 64.017 billion RMB, which was five times the total of the 25 years before the founding of the New China. Its proportion in total fixed asset investment increased from just 2-3% to 4%, China's infrastructural construction having thus begun to bottom out.[26]

---

[25] Jiang Shijie. *Investment in Infrastructure and Progress of Urbanization* [M]. Beijing: China Construction Industry Press, 2010

[26] Jiang Shijie. *Investment in Infrastructure and Progress of Urbanization* [M]. Beijing: China Construction Industry Press, 2010

3. Stage of Development from the 1990s to the Present Day

This stage witnessed a year-by-year increase in the share of social infrastructural investment, with remarkable achievements scored in infrastructural construction (see Figure 4-1). Considerable progress was made and a broad range of infrastructure was introduced for the first time in the country's history. Urban infrastructure was rolled out in a sustained manner that bolstered urbanization across the country.

Table 4-1 Development of urban infrastructure in China

Indexes	1990	1995	2000	2005	2010
Urban construction					
Built-up area (sq km)	12,856	19,264	22,439	32,521	40,058
Urban population density (people/sq km)	279	322	442	870	2,209
Urban supply of water, gas and central heating					
Aggregate annual water supply (bn m³)	38.23	48.16	46.9	50.21	50.79
Domestic water consumption (bn m³)	10.01	15.81	20	24.37	23.88
Domestic water per capita (tons)	67.9	71.3	95.5	74.5	62.6
Penetration of water supply (%)	48	58.7	63.9	91.1	96.7
Annual supply of manufactured gas (bn m³)	17.47	12.67	15.24	25.58	29.65
Household consumption (bn m³)	2.74	4.57	6.31	4.59	2.69
Annual supply of natural gas (bn m³)	6.42	6.73	8.21	21.05	48.76
Household consumption (bn m³)	1.16	1.64	2.48	5.21	11.72
Annual supply of LPG (mn tons)	2.19	4.887	10.537	12.22	12.68
Household consumption (mn tons)	1.428	3.702	5.323	7.065	6.339
Length of gas pipelines (1,000 km)	24	44	89	162	309
Penetration of gas supply (%)	19.1	34.3	45.4	82.1	92
Area of central heating (bn m³)	0.21	0.65	1.11	2.52	4.36
Municipal facilities					
Year-end length of constructed roads (1,000 km)	95	130	160	247	294
Road lengths per 1,000 people (km)	31	38	41	69	75
Lengths of urban drainage pipes (1,000 km)	58	110	142	241	370
Density of urban drainage pipes (km/km²)	4.5	5.7	6.3	7.4	9
Daily capacity of urban sewage treatment (mn m³)				79.897	133.929
Treatment rate of domestic sewage (%)				51.95	82.31
Urban public transport					
Year-end number of operating public transport vehicles (1,000 vehicles)	62	137	226	313	383

Indexes	1990	1995	2000	2005	2010
Public transport vehicles per 1,000 people (standard vehicles)	0.22	0.36	0.53	0.86	0.97
Total length of rail transit lines in operation (km^2)					1,428.9
Urban landscaping and gardening					
Area of urban green space (1,000 hectares)	475	678	865	1,468	
Per capita area of parks and greenbelt (m^2)	1.8	2.5	3.7	7.9	11.18
Numbers of parks	1,970	3,619	4,455	7,077	9,955
Area of parks (1,000 hectares)	39	73	82	158	258
Urban sanitation					
Delivering quantity of household refuse (mn tons)	67.67	106.71	118.19	155.77	158.05

Source: *China Statistical Yearbook 2007; China Construction Yearbook 2011*

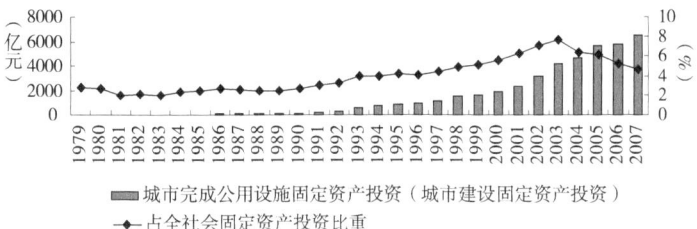

Figure 4-1 Percentage of investment in urban infrastructure (1979-2007)
Source: *China Urban Construction Statistics Yearbook*

Beginning in 2003, the country took the initiative to multiply government investment in basic industries and infrastructure, and encourage foreign and private capital to invest in projects that would enhance the construction of basic industries and infrastructure. The appearance of cities, the progress in urban economic and social development, and the quality of life of urban residents across the country were significantly improved. Between 2003 and 2007, the aggregate investment in basic industries and infrastructure reached 18.2703 trillion RMB. This was 1.6 times the level of the 1978-2002 period, the average annual growth rate having increased by 24.9% compared with a 9.2% rise in the overall national economy in the same period.[27]

During the 10th and 11th five-year plans, built-up urban infrastructure across the country grew to a considerable scale. According to the National Bureau of Statistics, the accumulated total completion of investment in China's urban infrastructural construction during the 11th Five-year Plan

---

[27] Jiang Shijie. *Investment in Infrastructure and Progress of Urbanization* [M]. Beijing: China Construction Industry Press, 2010

hit 22.1 trillion RMB. By exploiting major international events, such as the 2008 Olympic Games and the 2010 World Expo, Beijing, Shanghai and other super-large cities further developed their urban infrastructure and elevated urban functions.

With the constant improvement to hardware construction in urban infrastructure, software-related elements were also being developed. Meanwhile, reform in the system and mechanism of infrastructure continued to flourish, the centerpieces of which were the market orientation and separation of government functions from municipal public utilities in the infrastructure sector. Over the past two decades or so, all economic enterprises and institutions have jumped at the chance to invest in, or construct and develop, urban infrastructure. Meanwhile, there has been a proliferation in the number of specialized enterprises engaged in urban infrastructure and municipal public utilities. Simultaneously, the central and local governments have all drawn up and implemented catalogues of laws and regulations on urban infrastructure and public utilities concerning investment, construction, operation and supervision, thus ushering in China's national and local legal systems for the construction of urban infrastructure and public utilities (see Table 4-2).

Table 4-2 Laws and regulations related to drainage in Shanghai

Date of issue	Titles of laws, regulations and files	Contents	Notes
1995	Shanghai Municipal Administrations of Fees Paid for Drainage Facilities and Enforcement Regulations	Purpose, definition, application, competent authorities, collection and management authorities of drainage charge; computation, standard and way of charging	
1996	Regulations of Shanghai Municipality on Drainage Administration	Definition of drainage, drainage charge, supervision of the Water Supplies Bureau, reliability of districts and counties, duties of sewerage corporations, and accountability of governments at all levels and related departments in planning, construction, operation, management and maintenance	First issued in 1996 and amended three times in response to the reform of government's water affairs management system

2002	Provisional Regulations on the Management Liabilities of the City, Districts and Counties	Accountability of the Water Supplies Bureau in managing urban drainage inclusive of planning, supervision, approval, instruction and management of city and city-governed drainage facilities; competent departments at district and county levels responsible for planning, supervision, approval and reporting to higher authorities in managing city-owned and district-governed as well as district-owned and district-governed facilities	Adapted to the two-level coordinated management system between the city and subordinate districts
2011	Administrative Franchise of Shanghai Municipal Public Facilities	Franchising and authorized franchise through competition in operating and managing infrastructures	Exclusive of infrastructure in stock

II. Problems with the Construction of Urban Infrastructure in China

Although China has made impressive achievements in the construction and development of urban infrastructure and people have enjoyed ongoing improvements in their quality of life, we still have a long way to go in view of the mounting problems that confront us.

1. Asymmetry in Development

Despite the phenomenal progress in the development of urban infrastructure, China remains relatively behind in urban infrastructural construction considering the continuing acceleration of urbanization and residents' constantly growing demand for a better life. China is far behind highly urbanized countries and the world at large with regard to per capita indexes of most infrastructural facilities in light of the striking imbalance in the construction and development of its urban infrastructure. Such asymmetry refers to the disparities in regional distribution and the gulf between coastal regions and the interior. Second, it reflects the urban-rural disparity that exists due to the long-standing consideration that cities outweigh the countryside. Third, it relates to the fact that disequilibrium is found in the industrial structure of infrastructure and that the development of different infrastructural facilities varies considerably. For instance, in the 668 cities nationwide, about half of the built-up areas do not have a decent drainage system and are inflicted with inferior auxiliary facilities. This is particularly true in old urban districts where avenues are wide and a satisfactory plumbing system is absent, the penetration rate of drainage networks having stood merely at around 60%.[28]

2. Striking Financing Gaps

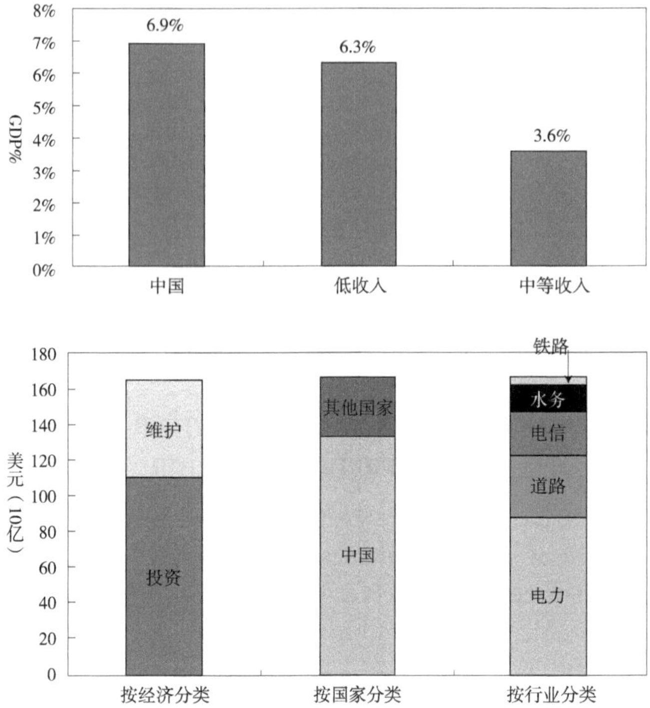

Figure 4-2 Prediction of demand for infrastructure investment in China

Source: ADB, JBIC & WB. *Connecting East Asia: A New Framework of Infrastructure* [M]. Beijing: World Bank Press, 2006

Studies by the Development Research Center of the State Council note that the most conservative estimate of investment in infrastructure for each increased urban resident will be 90,000 RMB. Findings by the United Nations Development Program show that investment in urban infrastructure in developing countries generally accounts for 3-5% of their GDP and the percentage will have to increase in line with an accelerating rate of urbanization. *Connecting East Asia: A New Framework of Infrastructure*, published by the Asian Development Bank, the Japan Bank for International

---

[28] Jiang Shijie. *Investment in Infrastructure and Progress of Urbanization* [M]. Beijing: China Construction Industry Press, 2010
[29] ADB, JBIC & WB. *Connecting East Asia: A New Framework of Infrastructure* [M]. Beijing: World Bank Press, 2006

Cooperation and the World Bank in 2006,[29] predicted that China's investment in infrastructure would reach approximately 7% of its annual GDP (see Figure 4-2). According to the estimate in the *Development Report on China's Urbanization* (2001-2002), an anticipated urbanization level of 70% in China by around 2050 will involve an investment of 40-50 trillion RMB in developing infrastructure, which means that an annual investment of 800-900 billion RMB will be needed. The financing of huge investment funds for infrastructure looms as a pressing issue to be addressed by the Chinese government.

3. System to Be Further Improved

Since 1999, the Chinese government has gradually relinquished control of its urban infrastructure market and brought into being a framework of diversified capital by introducing the competitive market mechanism and improving the system and mechanism for urban infrastructure investment, construction, operation and management.[30]

In July 2004, the State Council issued the *Decision on Reforming the Investment System* that encouraged and guided social capital to participate in constructing for-profit public welfare and infrastructural projects in the form of, for example, individual proprietorship, joint venture, cooperation, joint management and project financing. In February 2005, the State Council promulgated the *Suggestions on Encouraging, Supporting and Guiding the Development of Individual and Private Sectors and Other Non-public Economies* in which non-public capital was allowed to engage in public utility and infrastructure industries. It was stipulated that the government would accelerate the franchise system, regularize bidding behavior, and bolster non-public capital to energetically participate in investment in, as well as construction and operation of, the urban supply of water, gas and heating, public transportation, sewage and refuse disposal, and other municipal public utility and infrastructure projects. This package of policies and regulations helped promote the reform of urban infrastructural construction and the institutional mechanism of investment and financing, thereby bringing into being the fundamental role of the market in allocating resources.

With the accelerated marketization of infrastructure and pubic utilities after the 11th Five year Plan, problems such as lax government oversight

---

[30] Liao Maolin & Huang Yuhua. *Reform and Development of Investment and Financing System in China's Infrastructural Construction [A]. in China's Urbanization within Three Decades (1978-2008)* [C]. Beijing: Social Sciences Academic Press, 2009

arose along with alternative lines of thinking such as anti-marketization and de-marketization. However, the central government never changed its stance of driving the benign development of infrastructure and public utilities by bringing in the market mechanism, and instead it spared no effort in reforming and perfecting the institutional system of infrastructure and public utilities.

4. Deficiency in Maintenance

For quite some time, there has been a tendency to place a higher value on construction over maintenance with regard to urban infrastructure. Upon completion, many infrastructural facilities stay idle for a long time due to the absence of adequate regulations for maintenance. Several completed infrastructure facilities occasionally fail to be utilized on a sustained basis due to an acute lack of a mechanism to secure maintenance funds. Investigations found that the amount of public water supply facilities lying idle in some of China's municipal-level cities ranged from 20-50%. Of the 709 completed sewage treatment plants in China's 668 cities, only one-third are working normally, while one-third are under-utilized and the remaining one-third either operate only intermittently or remain idle. Inadequate maintenance of urban infrastructure will bring about inefficiency and a waste of infrastructure facilities, so much so that supplies of public services will be undermined. With the continuous acceleration of China's urbanization and the expansion of urban infrastructural construction, urban infrastructure facilities do require substantial maintenance. Provided that a stable and constant supply of funds for maintenance is absent and institutional arrangements for maintenance are unavailable, the operation of the infrastructure will be gravely affected to the point that even greater damage and waste will be caused.

III. Exploration into the Construction of Urban Infrastructure in China

1. Integration of Planning with the Market

Under a planned economy, infrastructure construction in China was controlled by the state and the government. Within the context of a socialist market economy, infrastructure construction and the development of municipal public utilities across the country was inseparable from the basic roles of government at all levels. Primary functions included investing part or all of the capital in infrastructure by using government funds, organizing and working out planning for urban infrastructure and industrial development along with the plan for implementation, formulating and improving the system, mechanism, laws and regulations for the marketization of infrastructure and municipal public utilities, arranging government bidding, implementing government procurement and transfer payments, coordinating public hearings, pricing municipal public services, and supervising and managing municipal public utilities.

In this regard, infrastructure and public utilities assume an organic and well-balanced combination of planning and marketing within the government-led framework that enables the government to play a basic and guiding role and puts to good use the market function of resource allocation so that enterprises will be able to compete effectively in a well-regulated market. China's experience has shown, time and again, that the government invariably plays the most crucial role where the market mechanism malfunctions, leaving the market and enterprises impotent in the infrastructure sector. When a favorable investment environment is created by the government to invigorate enterprises, the market and enterprises will further increase investment in, and development of, local infrastructure and public utilities to the extent that China's construction of urban infrastructure will gather pace and the development of urbanization and the regional economy will accelerate nationwide.

2. Integration of 'Soft Environment' with 'Hardware'

Since the central and local governments decided to accelerate the construction of urban infrastructure at the beginning of the 1980s, government sectors nationwide have all been keeping up with the times according to local circumstances. They not only gave preference to the construction of 'hardware infrastructure' but also woke up to the significance of driving an improvement of the 'software environment' in their efforts to pursue the principle of development that gives equal importance to both. Construction of the soft environment involves three aspects.

First, the emphasis on building up the external image of urban infrastructure has given way to a stress on improving the scope of public services. Today, policy priorities throughout the country have been shifted to how public service capacities of infrastructure can be improved rather than focused on the acceleration of infrastructure construction itself. The public disclosure of cost in water utilities is one example of government efforts to further the transparency of production and operation in public services.

Second, institutional establishment has been strengthened with the speeding up of construction of urban infrastructure, one of the major institutional orientations being the promotion of the function of market resource allocation. First, the reform of the financial investment system in the infrastructure sector has been carried out and the market has been progressively opened up with the introduction of the market mechanism in order that non-market capital will be invested in the construction of infrastructure. Second, the reform of the administrative system has been promoted in the field of infrastructure so that the role of the government will be transformed from administration to supervision of infrastructure and public utilities through separating enterprise from administration and the adoption of a franchise system in which the responsibilities of the government and enterprises in the investment in and construction and management of infrastructure will be clearly defined. In this way, construction and development of urban infrastructure will be stepped up with the gradual formulation and exercise of industrial policies, urban development plans, and laws and regulations that will help mobilize and motivate economic entities through guidance, management and regulation. Furthermore, the environment of market industrialization has been well cultivated in infrastructure so that all the various infrastructural enterprises will be energized to grow bigger and stronger. Government policies in this regard include the expansion of financing channels for infrastructural enterprises by encouraging them to be listed on the stock market, the elimination of unreasonable government administrative monopoly of enterprises by means of separating enterprise from administration, the encouragement of intra-industry mergers and integration of resources, the opening of regional markets and the promotion of cross-regional investment. The formulation and exercise of these policies has demonstrated that only market-oriented infrastructural enterprises will be able to develop wholesale and provide more and better public services for local municipal governments and communities.

Third, infrastructural construction and urbanization have been well integrated. Since infrastructural facilities in China are set up to serve both urban areas and rapid urbanization, infrastructure that is divorced from the development of cities is worthless and wasteful. In China's urbanization, therefore, the government must play a role in places where the market and enterprises are impotent so that government investment companies engaged in urban infrastructure will come into play. The increase in urban infrastructure investment has driven the revival of urban economic life and helped generate differential rents of urban land that will become the major source of revenue for local governments. As a result, the growth of the urban population and the local urban economy will be further quickened, to the extent that urbanization will in turn help promote the functions of infrastructure and the optimization of public services.

3. Integration of Innovation with Reality

Taking advantage of situations, acting according to circumstances, keeping up with the times and seizing the opportune moment to reform and innovate the institution, system and mechanism of infrastructure, and insisting on innovation in technology, management and concept are all pivotal to the construction and development of China's urban infrastructure. Construction of urban infrastructure, however, started at the primary stage of socialism that was falling behind economically and socially and was characterized by imbalanced regional development in which any innovative idea had to be realistic and pushed forward step by step according to real life conditions. For instance, the reform of Shanghai's urban infrastructure investment and financing system has stood the test of time because it did not materialize according to top-level design but was established after repeated trial and error along with the sustained deepening of reform in China's socialist market economy, the growing improvement of its financial and capital markets, and the mounting demand of its economic and social development (see Special Column 4-1). By contrast, some cities are blind to what is realistic in terms of speeding up infrastructural construction and expanding the scale of urban areas, resulting in investment bubbles in the infrastructure sector and the long-term waste of social and economic resources.

Special Column 4-1 Shanghai: urban construction and development[31]

Over the past three decades, the people of Shanghai, adhering to the ideological guideline of emancipating the mind and seeking truth from facts, and based on the realities of a country passing through the primary stage of socialism and with due consideration of what is distinctive in a super-large city, have acquired profitable experience and practices in urbanization.

1. Making urban construction the top strategic priority

Since the 1990s, urban construction has been given top priority for strategic development that is important for the overall reform and

---

[31] Chen Shijie, Feng Xiaomin & Luo Shiqian. *Urban Construction and Development in Shanghai* [M]. Shanghai: Shanghai People's Publishing House, 2004

progress of the city. The municipal government has been focusing on the concurrent and mutual development of economic growth, social advance and urban construction along with the unified arrangement and coordinated development of urban planning, construction and management, resulting in a significant increase in urban construction with a sustained growth in aggregate investment. Urban construction has created marked changes not only in the appearance of the city but also in its supply capacities and its multifunctional capabilities as well as in its overall economic activities. Studies suggest that urban construction was a major driving force behind the city's economic growth in the late 20th and early 21st century.

2. Scientific in planning and proactive in development

One of Shanghai's most important practices is to base urban construction and management on planning. The municipal government has insisted that urban planning is worked out in the first instance and, once this is done, specialized plans (including those of transportation, environment, water services, energy and information) will be able to relate to it so that a positive and proactive interaction between sectors can be achieved. The formulation of all plans along with the results of policy studies have played a guiding role par excellence in constructing specialized infrastructure.

3. Innovative, creative and pioneering

To substantially improve its inferior infrastructure, Shanghai has persisted in driving development by means of overall reform and innovation. The continuous intensification of the fundamental role of market resource allocation together with the constant resolution of relevant problems has lent powerful institutional support for rapid growth.

As regards the reform and innovation in urban construction and management, the highly-centralized urban construction system has gradually given way to the practices of 'two levels of government and three levels of administration' in urban areas and 'three levels of government and administration' in suburban counties. In both cases, the gravity of administration has shifted down.

In terms of the reform and innovation of public utilities, Shanghai has been pushing forward urban construction in a big way and in the process removed monopolized industries. From 1996-2000, Shanghai reformed the system, mechanism and fee scale of drainage, public transport, natural gas and water supply to form a market-orientated system of diversified investment and operation, and a comprehensive industrial management system.

Shanghai has all along been taking the lead nationally in the development of science and technological innovation. While forging ahead with large-scale urban construction, it has attached great importance to the role of scientific and technical innovation with the aim of improving the quality and efficiency of infrastructure construction by promoting scientific and technological progress. In the meantime, it has developed appropriate methods, standards and regulations and enhanced its modern urban administration by applying GPS information management, intelligent transportation systems, environmental biotechnology and other high-tech achievements to its urban and environmental management.

In terms of legal construction, Shanghai formulated and amended some 200 local laws and regulations that had significant bearing on urban construction and management between 1990 and 2004, of which around 90% were worked out based on the realities of the city. During the legislation process, stress was placed on the legislative program, preliminary investigation, adequate demonstration and all-inclusiveness. In operation, attention was paid to practicality, gradual accumulation and progressiveness in order to guarantee legislative quality and operability as well as the relative stability of local legislation. Insisting on administration and management according to the law, competent administrative departments were committed to promoting the effectiveness and efficiency of urban management with the help of legal and economic means.

Reform of both investment in urban infrastructure and financing systems is among the key government measures in its large-scale urban construction. By means of diversified and market-oriented investments and financing policies, such as inviting foreign capital, leasing land, issuing shares and bonds, collecting social funds, opening up the real estate market, making short-term loans from national financial institutions, and allocating social funds, Shanghai has addressed the problems with investment in urban construction and brought down the cost of financing, construction and operation.

In this way it has significantly improved the economic efficiency and social benefit of investment.

4. Social participation and public support

The big expansion in urban construction in Shanghai is inseparable from the substantial support and assistance of society, one prominent aspect of which is diversified financing. Mindful of the overall interests and practical realities of their city, residents have contributed greatly to urban construction with their understanding and support. Given the sustained deepening of urban construction and growing extent of demolition in Shanghai, the government has had to enlist the understanding, support and cooperation of citizens. It adheres to the principles of wholeheartedly serving the people, helping to alleviate their hardships, doing what is good and pragmatic for their benefit, and providing them with timely help. In practice, it sticks to the belief that the public must be well informed when major reform policies are carried out so that they will offer support and engage themselves in the operation. With regard to reform proposals that involve wide public interests, the government calls on the people to contribute ideas and work to win their understanding and support. As for emerging problems in urban construction, particularly those that cause frequent arguments among citizens, it tries to assess the situation so that it will be able to provide timely guidance and prevent potential problems from occurring.

Chapter 5

Management of Urban Land in China

I. Property Rights of Urban Land

As the centerpiece of the land system and basis of agrarian relations, land ownership implies an economic form in which one owns land under certain social conditions. Accordingly, property rights of land, as the legal manifestation of land ownership, constitutes the legally protected exclusive and proprietary right of land owners that can be broken down into the right to use, the right to earnings, the right of disposition and so on. As is specified in the *Law of the PRC on Land Administration*, China practices the socialist public ownership of land, which involves ownership by the whole people and collective ownership by the working people. It further stipulates: "Land in urban areas of a city shall be owned by the state. Land in rural and suburban areas of a city shall be owned by a farmer collective, except for that which belongs to the state as provided for by law; housing sites and private plots of cropland and hilly land are owned by a farmer collective."

The land-use system that serves to stipulate the procedures, conditions and forms of land utilization is another key component of the land system. The right to the use of land is a legal manifestation that enables land owners to enjoy the right to use, manage and gain profit from land. The reform of the property right system of land in China mainly focuses on the institutional innovation of the right to the use of land.

After the PRC was founded, the system of land property in cities shifted from private ownership to state ownership. Before 1949, when private ownership of land was practiced, urban land in China accounted for a very insignificant share of the country's total territorial area and it was largely occupied by the bureaucratic bourgeoisie feudal landlords, national industrialists and merchants, self-employed laborers and foreigners. With the founding of the new China, municipal governments across the country took over the land previously owned by the Kuomintang government and confiscated extensive tracts of urban land occupied by imperialists and bureaucrat bourgeoisies. Official recognition was given to private land belonging to national industrialists and merchants, along with self-employed laborers and urban residents.

At the nascent stage of China's urban construction, therefore, there was a co-existence of state and private ownership of urban land. The owners of private urban land were not conferred the right to freely dispose of their own land until 1956. In the *Opinions on the Basic State and Socialist Reform of Current Private Urban Real Estate* issued on January 18, 1956, the Secretariat of the CPC Central Committee stipulated that all unused private-owned urban land and other real estate should be nationalized by appropriate means and that state-owned urban land should be allocated to land users free of rent by local governments[32] so as to bring into being the urban land-use system along with the overall nationalization of urban land ownership. In line with the system, the use of state-owned urban land would be free of charge, open-ended and non-liquid. The system of free allocation of state-owned urban land brought the integrated proprietorship and usufruct of land entirely under the control of the state.[33]

Despite the fact that the administrative allocation system of state-owned land was adapted to the development mode of the planned economy stage, growing problems became apparent: inefficiency of utilization, a severe waste of land resources, failure in economic realization of the ownership of state-owned land and an acute depletion of the rights to earnings and free disposition.

With the deepening of reform in China's economic system and opening up to the outside world, the national economic system was crackling with dynamic changes. A number of innovative initiatives were introduced because the previous system of land use had failed to keep up with the steps of reform and opening up. The institutional innovation of China's urban land use during the period largely found expression in the establishment of the paid use system of urban land based on notional rent.

---

[32] Bi Baode. *Studies on the Real Estate Market in China* [M]. Beijing: China Renmin University Press, 1994, page 27

[33] Dong Liming. *Review and Prospects for Paid Use of Urban Land in China* [J]. Yunnan Geographic Environment Research, 1992, (12), pages 16-29

1. Charges and Taxes on Land Use

(1) Charges on land use

The reform of China's urban land-use system first took place in the land-use system for Sino-foreign joint ventures. In 1979, the State Council promulgated the *Law of the PRC on Chinese-Foreign Equity Joint Ventures*, which stipulated that the investment contributed by a Chinese party could include the right to the use of premises provided for the equity joint venture during the period of its operation; in case such a contribution did not constitute a part of the investment from the Chinese party, the venture should pay the Chinese government a fee for its use of the land. The *Provisional Regulations on Land for Construction by the Sino-foreign Equity Joint Ventures* issued by the State Council on July 26, 1980, specified that occupancy fees should be levied on land for Sino-foreign equity joint ventures, whether it was newly requisitioned land or the land of original enterprises. These laws, regulations and policies helped change the situation with the uncompensated use of urban land in China, thereby initiating the reform in the urban land-use system. In 1982, Shenzhen started to collect land occupancy charges and more than 100 cities across the country followed suit from 1998.

(2) Taxes on land use

In compliance with the *Tentative Regulations of the PRC on Urban Land-use Taxes* promulgated by the State Council on September 7, 1988, collection of urban land-use taxes would start from November 1, 1988. The central government would be responsible for levying taxes on domestic users of land while regional and municipal governments would take charge of gathering land-use taxes on foreign-invested enterprises as well as overseas companies' institutions based in China. With this, China finished establishing its legal system that featured paid or compensated use of urban land.

2. Establishment of the Urban Land Transfer System

Although the exercise of collecting charges and taxes on land users broke away from the previous system of uncompensated use of land and supplied valuable experience for the reform of the land-use system, it failed to touch upon the innovation of the land market mechanism. With the growing scale of urban construction, problems with the allocation of land resources raised government concern. As the tax rate standard stipulated was under par, the fees collected fell far short of meeting the demand of infrastructure construction. While land developers made easy and fast money, the ownership of the government as the representative holder of state-owned land failed to materialize economically. Moreover, collection of meager fees for the right to the use of land alone could not help promote the rational allocation of land resources and the efficient utilization of urban land. Although departments responsible for the administrative allocation of land strove to be impartial in their initial assignment, they still found that efficient use of land responsive to market signals was elusive due to the absence of necessary competition and economic levers coupled with a failure of the right to the use of land to enter the market for legal negotiation and mortgage. In this context, it was imperative to carry out a more profound and larger-scale reform in the land-use system.

Taking the lead in innovating the land-use system, Shenzhen tentatively separated the ownership of land from the right to use land. Based on the prerequisite that urban land is state owned, the government leased the right to its use by means of open bid and tender. On September 9 and 29 and November 1, 1987, the municipal government broke through the legal binding on the right to the use of urban land and became a national pacesetter in allocating land resources by means of the market when it leased the right to the use of three plots of state-owned land through agreement, open bidding and public tender. In November 1987, with the approval of the State Council, pilot reform of land use was conducted in Shenzhen, Shanghai, Tianjin, Guangzhou, Xiamen and Fuzhou, the essence of it being that the right to the use of administratively allocated land that had been free of charge, open-ended and non-negotiable was going to be paid, time-limited and negotiable.

This practical development entailed the modification of relevant laws. In April 1988, the National People's Congress amended the constitution by removing the previous stipulation that land was not negotiable and inserting "the right to the use of land may be negotiated according to law". Afterwards, corresponding modifications were made to the PRC's Land Administration Law, thereby creating the legal basis for the leasing and negotiation of the right to use state-owned land. In the *Interim Regulations of PRC Concerning the Leasing and Negotiation of the Right to the Use of State-owned Land in Urban Areas* issued in May 1990, the State Council expressly defined the leasing, negotiation, renting, mortgage and termination of the right to the use of state-owned land. The *Law of the PRC on Urban Real Estate Administration*, promulgated in 1994, explicitly stipulated the state-practiced system of using state-owned land under due compensation and terms of using the land according to the law. In 1998, the amended *Administration Law of the PRC* further stipulated that the right to the use of land might be leased by law, that the state introduced the system of compensated use of land owned by the state and that paid leasing should apply in use of land owned by the state by a construction unit. These issued and implemented laws and regulations have constituted the system of land-use rights composed of a package of legal documents consisting of the *Real Right Law of the PRC*, the *Land Administration Law of the PRC*, the *Law of the PRC on Urban Real Estate Administration*, the *Law of the PRC on Land Contract in Rural Areas*, the *Provisions on the Leasing of State-owned Construction Land Use Right through Bid Invitation, Auction and Quotation*, and others that have brought into being the basic institutional framework of the market operation of state-owned land as well as the land property right system with Chinese characteristics.

II. Utilization and Management of Urban Land

Administration of land use is a manifestation of national intervention for all the processes of land use so that the state will better organize and utilize land. Administration of land use in China mainly involves administration of land-use plans, land-use planning, land consolidation as well as purposes of land use. Since the reform and opening up was launched, China, based on its own national realities, has established the administrative system of land use singular to itself.

1. Protection of Cultivated Land

The protection of cultivated land is a top priority in land management and the centerpiece of land use administration. In March 1986, the Central Committee of the CPC and the State Council jointly promulgated the *Notice on Strengthening Land Administration and Curbing Unlawful Appropriation of Cultivated Land* in which the basic policy of the state was referenced for the first time: "Every inch of land shall be treasured and rationally utilized for protecting cultivated land." In August 1994, the issuing of the *Regulations on the Protection of Basic Farmland* by the State Council signified that protection of basic farmland was officially brought under the control of legal regulation. The *Land Administration Law of the PRC*, amended in 1999, established two policy frameworks for protecting cultivated land in China: a balance system of the total amount of cultivated land and a land-use control system. The introduction of the two policies signaled that the focus of land management had shifted from securing the supply of land for construction to protecting cultivated land, or from a batch-wise approval limit system (see Special Column 5-2) to a land-use control system.[34]

(1) Establishing a strict land-use control system

The land-use control system is extensively adopted in countries and regions across the world where the land management system is relatively well developed. In this system, the government, for the purpose of securing rational utilization of land resources in promoting the coordinated development of the economy, society and environment, works out land-use planning, stipulates the uses of land, defines the prerequisites for land use, and demands that all land owners and users utilize land in strict compliance with the uses and preconditions specified in the planning. The Chinese government hopes that the exercise of a land-use control system will provide strict protection for cultivated land.

(2) Intensifying the balance system of total amount of cultivated land

The balance system of the total amount of cultivated land, which is otherwise referred to as dynamic balance means of total arable land, is a central system designed to counteract the reduction of total arable land by adopting measures to secure an area of cultivated land adequate for the demands of social and economic development within a certain period of time. Articles 31 and 32 of the *Land Administration Law of the PRC* explicitly stipulate that the state fosters a system of compensation for the occupation of cultivated land. In the case of occupying cultivated land for non-agricultural construction, the units occupying cultivated land should be responsible for reclaiming the same amount of land in the same quality as that occupied according to the principle of 'reclaiming the same amount of land occupied'. Governments of all provinces, autonomous regions and municipalities shall strictly implement the general planning for the utilization of land and annual planning for the use of land and adopt measures that do not lead to a reduction in the total amount of cultivated land within their jurisdictions. When reductions occur, the State Council shall order land reclamation within a prescribed time limit

---

[34]Land-use control system, the centerpiece of China's land management system, stipulates that governments at all levels are responsible for formulating the master planning for land use that defines the uses of land by classifying them into agricultural land, land for construction and unused land. The owners and users of land shall use the land in strict compliance with the purposes of use prescribed by the state. The government imposes a strict restriction on turning farmland into land for construction, controls the quantum of construction land and provides special protection for cultivated land. Structural adjustment of agriculture and development of protected agriculture will be promoted by making the most of barren mountains, waste hillsides, intertidal zones and other unused lands of low profit without occupying cultivated land, prime farmland in particular.

to make up for the diminished land in the same quantity and quality, and the land administrative department of the State Council shall, together with the agricultural administrative department, examine and accept it.

Apart from these two measures, China also exercises strict control over the scale of urban land and strengthens the protection of cultivated land through the improvement of farmland quality and the establishment of detecting systems for the dynamic protection of arable land.

2. Planning and Enforcement of Land Use

In the *Land Administration Law of the PRC* issued in June 1986, people's governments at all levels were required to compile general plans for land uses. In accordance with the stipulation of this law, China restructured the classification system of land, worked out national general land planning for 2000, 2010 and 2020, formulated the top-down five-level overall planning system encompassing the state, provinces, cities, counties and townships, completed the optimal allocation of the scale, structure, spatial layout, intensity and time sequence of land use, realized the balance between varieties of land, protected arable land, promoted the development and utilization of inefficient and unused land resources, and satisfied the demand for construction purposes. In the meantime, it carried out in a comprehensive way the planning for the protection of prime farmland, for land consolidation, and for development and reclamation of land. It also formulated the annual planning for land use (inclusive of targets for non-agricultural construction) (see Special Column 5-1) and the control system of land uses.

Special Column 5-1 Management of land-use planning

By means of management of land-use planning, a macro-control measure adopted by the state to address all eventualities in land use, the state works out planning and issues control targets so that it can guide people to use land in a planned and rational way and in doing so it brings land use into the system of national planning management. Management of land-use planning mainly includes the formulation of plans, issuing of targets and implementation of plans. The plans comprise medium- and long-term plans for land use as well as an annual plan for construction land; the targets primarily refer to arable land for various construction purposes issued by the state each year as well as those of land for other uses; and implementation involves the exercise, inspection and summarization of plans. Put another way, local land administrations at all levels first propose the targets of land use before reporting, level by level, to the next superior administration. With balanced consideration, the national land administrations and planning departments draw out the plan in line with which the targets are allocated to each province before transmitting the control targets to governments at higher levels. In compliance with the control targets of land use, the local land administrations modify the previously suggested number of targets of land use before reporting once again to administrations at higher levels. With the approval of the central government, the planned targets are conclusively assigned to each subordinate government, level by level.

3. Management of Land for Construction

Land for construction refers to land exclusively used for specific project building and resource development by means of certain material input and engineering measures. Land for construction, according to its purpose of use, breaks down into land for agricultural construction and land for non-agricultural construction, of which the latter is further classified into land for state construction, land for construction of townships (towns) and land for construction by foreign-invested enterprises (FIEs) in accordance with the proprietorship, the source of investment and the uses of land. Land for urban construction chiefly consists of land for state construction and land for construction by FIEs.

Land for state construction refers to that used for developing a country's economy, culture, national defense and public utilities, including land for urban construction, industry and mining, transportation, irrigation and other specially-designated purposes.

Land for construction by FIEs refers to that used for production and engineering construction by Sino-foreign equity joint ventures, Chinese-foreign cooperative ventures and foreign-funded enterprises.

(1) Management of land for state construction

Land for state construction comes from two major sources: requisitioned land collectively owned in rural areas and allocated state-owned land. It can also be acquired by means of leasing or negotiation.

Land requisition is a process by which collectively-owned land is transformed into state-owned land according to law, responsive to the needs of economic and cultural construction, building of national defense, and the establishment of social and public welfare.

The allotment of the right to use land is an act in which a plot of land, with the approval of the people's government above county level according to law, is consigned to the land user for use after they have paid the required compensation and settlement fees, or the right to the use of the land is consigned to the land user for uncompensated use with the approval of the people's government above county level according to law.

Leasing of the right to the use of land is an act in which the state leases, within a term of years, the right to use state-owned land to land users who have paid the state leasing fees for the right to the use of land. Land users who have acquired the right to the use of land through leasing are entitled to the negotiation, rent and mortgage of the right to the use of land as well as other activities for business purposes within the prescribed time.

In agreement with the *Regulations on the Implementation of the Land Administration Law of the PRC*, the examination and approval of land for state construction involves the following procedures:

A. A construction unit proposing to use land for construction purposes shall apply to the land administration department of the local people's government at county level or above in the locality of the land it wants to expropriate by presenting an approved design assignment or other relevant documents such as preliminary designs or annual capital construction plans.

B. The land administration department of the local people's government at county level or above shall examine the application to use land for construction purposes and determine the boundaries of the area of land to be used, as well as arrange for the construction unit, the unit that formerly held the rights to the land and other relevant units to discuss matters of compensation and resettlement in relation to the expropriated land and report these particulars to the people's government at county level or above for approval.

C. After the application to the land for construction purposes is approved by the relevant people's government at county level or above pursuant to the statutory approval jurisdiction, the people's government at county level or above in the locality of the expropriated land shall issue a document of approval to use the land for construction purposes and the land administration department shall transfer the land-use rights in full or in stages, depending on the construction schedule.

D. Upon completion of construction, when the department in charge of the construction project arranges for relevant authorities to examine construction prior to acceptance of the project, the land administration department of the people's government at county level or above shall inspect and verify the actual use of the land (after completion of a construction project in an urban planning district, the administrative authority in charge of urban planning shall, in conjunction with the land administration department, inspect and verify the actual use of the land) and, subject to confirmation, land registration procedures shall be carried out and a land-use certificate for state-owned land shall be issued.

(2) Management of land for construction by FIEs

At present, the acquisition of land by FIEs mainly includes compensated transfer of the right to use state-owned land, allocation of the right to use land, utilization of the right to use state-owned land as the condition for cooperation as well as leasing of houses and premises.

A. Leasing of the right to use state-owned land

Leasing of the right to use state-owned land is an act in which the state leases the right to use state-owned land within a term of years to foreign-funded enterprises that have paid the state the leasing fees for land-use rights in full. The leasing of land-use rights is generally achieved by means of auction, invitation for bids or mutual agreement. In many places, it is stipulated that FIEs engaged in for-profit projects such as real estate development, commerce, tourism, entertainment and construction of luxury homes have to acquire land-use rights by means of leasing.

B. Allocation of the right to use state-owned land

With the approval of people's government above county level according to law, foreign-funded enterprises can enter into land-use contracts with the land administration departments of local cities and counties, pay land occupancy charges as stipulated, carry out land registration procedures and acquire certificates for the right to use state-owned land that they are not entitled to negotiate, mortgage or rent.

C. The right to use state-owned land as the condition for cooperation

As is stipulated by the state, a Chinese party, after going through land-use procedures in the land administration departments above county level, may have its plant, equipment and land-use rights evaluated in lieu of shares as the condition for establishing joint or cooperative ventures with foreign enterprises. When the right to use land is administratively allocated as the condition for cooperation, the Chinese party of the joint and cooperative venture shall pay land-use fees annually as stipulated.

D. Renting of houses and premises

When a foreign-funded enterprise rents houses or premises directly from state-owned or collective economic entities or from township enterprises or the army, it shall pay rent to the leasers annually in accordance with the provisions of their contracts.

4. Management of Land for Industry

To further economic progress, China has introduced its *sui generis* system and policies for development zones, making possible the centralized and efficient allocation of land for secondary industry. However, all places across the country, for the purpose of attracting investment, used to lease land at a low price and even free of charge to the extent that many inferior projects were launched blindly, land resources were squandered and a huge quantity of land assets were lost. For this reason, the State Council issued the *Decision on Deepening Reform and Intensifying Land Administration* in October 2004, which stipulated that conditions should be created for industrial land to be allocated or leased equally by means of invitation for bids, auction and price-listing so that the market-based allocation of land resources would be promoted. Before the promulgation of the policy, the practice of 'project approval prior to supply of land' was predominant in assigning land for industrial construction. That is to say, the scale of land use was determined in accordance with the land-use index for project construction or engineering design specification. In September 2006, the State Council issued the *Circular on Intensifying Land Control* in which the policy of 'land prior to project' was established when it stressed that leasing of the right to the use of industrial land must be exercised in line with the lowest price standard and that industrial land should be exclusively leased by means of invitation for bids, auction and price-listing. Beginning from 2007, with the implementation of the *National Standards for the Minimum Leasing Prices of Land for Industrial Purposes*, the minimum price standard for industrial land leasing was defined.

On October 1, 2009, the Ministry of Land and Resources, with the aim to further carry out the *State Council's Approval and Forwarding of the Opinions of the National Development and Reform Commission and Other Departments on Restraining Overcapacity and Repeated Construction of Some Industries and Guiding Them to Embark on a Healthy Development*, promulgated a catalog of projects for which land was limited (supplement edition of 2006) and the catalog of projects for which land is prohibited (supplement edition of 2006) so as to promote industrial restructuring as well as the economical and intensive utilization of land. Accordingly, Shanghai and some other cities, in order to perfect the management system of industrial land, formulated and enacted a series of enforcement regulations and administrative standards, including the *Trial Measures of Shanghai City for Control and Management of Land-Use Scale in Approving Construction Projects*, the *Guide for Industrial Land Use in Shanghai City* (editions 2004 and 2006), the *Guide for Industrial Orientation and Layout in Shanghai*, the *Guideline for Supply of Industrial Land in Shanghai* (trial version), and the *Price Standards for Leasing Industrial Land in Shanghai*.

Special Column 5-2 Multistory standard plants built in Shangyu for enhancing the effective use of industrial land

In its effort to press ahead with the public leasing of land for standard industrial plants and the construction of standard plants, Shangyu city has stood out as a trailblazer in the economical and intensive utilization of land. In order to break through the constraints of land on economic growth and set up a platform for small and medium-sized enterprises by means of intensive utilization of land, in 2005 the city decided to construct standard plants as the best solution to problems with industrial land. The government stipulated that all projects with a planning area below 10 mu (1.6 acres) and an investment of less than 10 million RMB would be settled exclusively with standard plants instead of an assignment of land. From 2005 to the end of April 2007, the city leased a total of 258 acres of land for standard plants, and finished constructing 1.4m square yards of multistory standard plants that attracted 145 small and medium-sized enterprises.

To drive the construction of multistory standard plants and encourage small and medium-sized enterprises to have access to them, the government has adopted incentives as follows: first, priority is given to projects related to standard plants; second, enterprises engaged in the construction of standard plants are rewarded and subsidized; and third, enterprises that have settled down in standard plants are rewarded and subsidized.

All standard plants engineered and constructed in Shangyu are above four floors with a plot ratio of more than 1.3 and a site coverage of at least 35%, the investment intensity having reached more than 1.35 million RMB per mu (about 800 square yards). The ratio of green space has been held within 15%, the proportion of living and administrative facilities has been controlled below 7% and the floor area of living and administrative facilities has been kept within 15%. The popularity of multistory standard plants has helped promote the intensive utilization of land.

Source: Li Feng & Qiu Jianyong. *The Win-win 'Project Number One' – Insight into the Rapid Construction of Multistory Standard Plants in Shangyu City* [J]. *China Land*, 2007 (6)

III. Management of the Urban Land Market
1 Current State of the Urban Land Market

China's land market currently comprises the market for leasing the right to use state-owned land and the market for negotiating the right to use state-owned land.

(1) Market for leasing the right to use state-owned land

In this market, the state transfers with compensation land-use rights to land users. At the market for leasing the right to use state-owned land, the land owner, namely the state, may lease land-use rights to organs, enterprises, public institutions or individuals by means of agreements, invitation for bids, auction and so on. What is transacted on the market is not the ownership or proprietorship of land but the use right within a given period of time. Moreover, rights are limited to land surface rather than underground natural resources, minerals, buried objects or hidden property. When the term of land-use rights expires and the contract is not renewed, the land owner shall reclaim the land-use rights together with above-ground structures. There are two means of market transaction for leasing land-use rights. The first is the long-term leasehold of land-use rights that meets the long-standing demand of land for which the tenure can be determined in line with the earnings and actual needs of the manufacturing industries and projects in operation. In China, the maximum terms of tenancy are: seven decades for residential land; five decades for industrial land; five decades for land for the purposes of education, science and technology, culture, public health and sports; four decades for commercial, tourist and recreational land; and five decades for commercial-residential land and others. The current maximum terms of leasing are legally stipulated by the State Council and specific provisions have been drawn up in individual places. The second means, which extends from one to 10 years, is the short-term leasehold of land-use rights that satisfies temporary or short-term needs.

Generally, a variety of provisions and qualifications will be attached to the leasing of land-use rights. These provisions and qualifications enable municipal governments to stipulate and carry out the overall design of social and economic development and land-use planning by means of legally-bound leasing contracts. Leasing contracts are covenants or agreements struck up between the land owner and lessees. Contracts should comprise the rights to which the lessees are entitled, the obligations they shall assume and the terms they must observe, including the duration of leasing, purposes of leasing, development types, building height, site coverage, ratio of floor area, minimum investment and requirement for public facilities. Any change in the purpose of land use must receive government approval and the parties involved will have to make good the stipulated price differences. The retransfer of land-use rights within a leasehold shall not be allowed until a change of registration is carried out in accordance with relevant provisions. The government is entitled to punish those breaching the contract.

The market for leasing land-use rights has three main features. First, though it is a market where land-use rights are transacted, the ownership of land is not lost after the buyer pays the premium and acquires the right to the use of land within a certain period of time while the seller receives the premium and loses land-use rights for the time being. Second, the land price is the purchase price of land-use rights within a given period of time, of which the basic components include absolute rent, differential rent and land interest on capital. Third, it is a market featuring monopoly and competition, the leaser of land-use rights being the state and the national department of land administration monopolizing land supplies at the market on behalf of the government. Land users are permitted to vie with one another through various competitive means for the right to use land.

(2) Market for negotiating the right to use state-owned land

The market for the negotiation of land-use rights is where the right to use land is negotiated between land users. If the former land user intends to transfer the land-use rights to another party, the duration of the new agreement shall not exceed the term of the contract struck between the former land user and the land owner. In this case, the negotiation of land-use rights will be considered illegal and punished according to law unless it is conducted under the supervision of the land administration department of the government.

During the negotiation of land-use rights, the former land user breaks off relations with the land owner through the transfer of overall land-use rights for a certain duration to a new land user. In doing so, relations between them and the land owner in terms of rights and obligations are simultaneously passed on to the new land user. Such a transaction follows the principle of 'priority of land over people', which means that a unit or individual is not only entitled to the rights and interests of land and housing estates but also assumes the liabilities and responsibilities regarding land disposal and real estate the moment they take over the land-use rights or real estate. In this regard, the exercise of 'priority of land over people' guarantees that the rights of the government and other units or individuals will not be negatively affected by repeated negotiations of land-use rights and real estate. In the final analysis, during the transfer or negotiation of land-use rights, the party involved shall pay the state value-added taxes on the land.

Negotiation of land-use rights has three main features. First, economic and legal relationships are more complicated since they involve relations between land users as well as economic and legal relationships between land users and the land owner. Second, the result of the transaction is a lateral flow of land-use rights, which helps to overcome the limitations of the longitudinal flow of leased land-use rights on the land market, eradicate land vacancy, promote the efficiency of land use and facilitate the rational allocation of land resources. Third, it is a well administered competitive market where competition for land-use rights exists on the supply side while potential users vie for the right to the use of land. In this light, the basis of price or leasing price of land-use right is increasingly brought under the regulation of the law of value and of land supply and demand.

The markets of leasing and negotiation of land-use rights that are reciprocally complemented and organically integrated constitute China's overall land market pattern.

2 Aspects and Modes of Urban Land Market Management

(1) Basic contents and modes in urban land market management

Land is a central factor of production and an important resource that can be controlled and regulated by the government. Based on its overall goals of social and economic development, the government intervenes in the urban land market by comprehensively applying economic and administrative means so that it can restrict land speculation, maintain the stability of the land market, optimize the management of land resources and distribute land revenues rationally.

A. Macro-management of the land market

By means of macro-management of the land market, the state, based on its long-term overall goals of social and economic development, intervenes in the urban land market through economic means (including industrial policies, finance and credit policies, and tax policies) and administrative measures (including plans and planning) so as to restrain land speculation, maintain the stability of the land market, optimize the allocation of land resources and distribute land revenues rationally. Macro-management of the land market comprises management of land market supply and demand, and control of land market prices.

B. Micro-management of the land market

Through micro-management, the state exercises unified regulation and management of the land market by applying legal and administrative means and measures so that it can ensure fair trade and competition between market entities and give play to the normal regulating functions of the land market mechanism.

(2) Regulation and management of land market supply and demand

As an important means to optimize the allocation of land resources and rationally distribute land revenues, regulation of land market supply and demand is conducive to the stability of land and housing prices as well as the adjustment and optimization of land-use structure.

A. Major contents of the regulation of land market supply and demand

i) Regulation orientation of land market supply and demand

The regulation orientation of land supply and demand involves opting for regulation goals and determining the operation orientation of regulating measures. The selection of regulation goals hinges on the development goals of the land market within a given period of time. In determining the operation orientation of regulating measures, the prevailing condition of the land market will have to be analyzed based on regulation goals. The operation orientation is roughly divided into two types: one is associated with the incentives adopted to stimulate the development of the land market, of which the operation is oriented upward and manifests as tax reduction and exemption, reduction of loan interest rates and so on; another has much to do with the measures taken to restrain the development of the land market, of which the operation is oriented downward and is evident in the control of loan sizes, the limitation of land supply and others. In general, the upward operation orientation is exercised as a regulating measure during the business cycle of the land market between depression and recovery, while the downward operation orientation is adopted when the land market is thought to be 'overheating'.

ii) Regulation time of land market supply and demand

To determine the regulation time of land market supply and demand, three parameters have to be taken into account: the decision-making time of regulation measures for supply and demand; the delayed time for the regulating effect of supply and demand; and the inertia of the regulating effect. The regulation of urban land market supply and demand must be combined with the improvement of the monitoring and warning system of the land market.

iii) Regulation intensity of land market supply and demand

The intensity or dimension of regulation is associated with a change in the variables that function as regulating measures. In this respect, four factors have to be considered: the extent of the economic fluctuation of land; the delayed time of the regulating measures from initiation to the moment when effect is generated; the scale of the inertia of the regulating effect; and the environment of regulation.

B. Measures for regulating land market supply and demand

– Development planning and formulation of land-use planning, notably annual planning, constitute the effective means to regulate the land market and determine the time for land to enter the market. Land-use planning functions as the key government measure to harness land supply, coordinate supply and demand, regulate and stabilize land prices and ultimately impose macro-regulation on the land market.

– Fiscal policies. Fiscal polices for the regulation of land market supply and demand include those of rent, tax and financial investment, and they play vital roles in regulating the speed of land market development as well as supply and demand dynamics. Tax policy functions in regulating land market supply and demand as follows: first, it regulates the land market by means of taxation in different operating links of the market; and second, it regulates the land market through tax relief. The policy of financial investment plays a role in directing financial investment by guiding social investment with financial investment so as to regulate industrial structure and regional disparities.

– Financial policies. Financial policies play a crucial part in the government's regulation of land market supply and demand. The regulatory functions of financial policies in regulating the land market fall into direct and indirect regulations. By virtue of direct regulation, the government, relying on the central bank, directly intervenes in the quality and quantity of land credit business through formulating land financial policies. Indirect regulation means that the state controls land market supply and demand by regulating the supply and demand of money by virtue of the interest rate, loan-to-value ratio and other financial levers.

(3) Macro-management and innovative management of the urban land market – the land reservation system

The land reservation system exists when the government is engaged in preliminary land development, consolidation and reservation in line with the overall planning of land use and urban planning through acquisition of the ownership and right to use land in its application of the market mechanism according to law so that it will be able to supply the land demanded in urban construction and regulate the management system and operating mechanism of the land market.

In terms of operation, the system of land acquisition and reservation primarily consists of land acquisition, land reservation and land supply.

A. Land acquisition

Land acquisition is an act in which land reserve institutions purchase or reclaim the right to use state-owned land within urban areas with the authorization of municipal governments and in accordance with land reserve plans. The procedures generally include application for acquisition, verification of ownership, consultation, expenditure measurement, submission and approval, compensation for acquisition, change in ownership and handover of land. In general, compensation for land acquisition is calculated according to the development cost of the land acquired. In cases where the right to use land is acquired through leasing, compensation should also include the sum for the previously paid leasing fees by land users though the leasing fees should be paid by the former land users for their actual use of the land.

B. Land reservation

Before it is leased to other land users, the land that has entered the reserve system shall be organized by land reserve centers for preliminary development, operation and management.

C. Land supply

With regard to land that has entered the reserve system, land reserve institutions are responsible for formulating supply plans and providing land for land users according to the needs of urban development and land market demand. In agreement with current provisions of land management, the supply of reserved land breaks down into leasing through invitation for bid, auction and price-listing and leasing by means of agreement.

In its effort to adapt to industrial restructuring, activate reserved urban land assets, optimize distribution of land resources and promote government regulation of the land market, the State Council promulgated in April 2001 the *Notice on Strengthening the Administration of State-owned Land Assets*. The notice stated that the governments of cities where conditions permitted should exercise a pilot system of land acquisition and reservation in order to strengthen the government's ability to regulate the land market. Governments at city and county levels could set aside some land revenues to provide credit aid for the acquisition of land and financial institutions. Subsequently, most cities across the country started to establish their own land reserve institutions and push ahead with the construction of land reserve systems. China's urban land reservation has three main features.

i) Market-based model

Land acquisition and reserve institutions, in accordance with the proposed plans for acquisition and government requirements, conduct evaluation of the land to be acquired and negotiate the acquisition price or gainshare with former land users before paying them the fees for acquisition, acquiring the land and carrying out the transfer procedures according to current provisions. Land reserve institutions are responsible for demolishing, consolidating and constructing supporting facilities before the land is leased to new land users by land administration departments.

ii) Government-led model

The scope of land acquisition is stipulated by the government's administrative laws and regulations. The land within the defined scope shall be purchased, reserved and developed by land reserve institutions commissioned by the government. Land administration departments, in line with the demand for land, are responsible for leasing the reserved land by means of invitation for bid, auction and price-listing.

iii) Combined mode of government leadership and market operation

This mode mainly applies to the acquisition and reservation of land appropriated during the reform of state-owned enterprises. The previously negotiated land that is publicly tradable with government approval, for which the land users have made good the leasing fees and readjusted the uses of the land in conformity with the overall planning, can either be acquired by land acquisition and reserve institutions or publicly traded on the land market.

Chapter 6

Management of Urban Communities

I. Evolution of the Urban Community Management System

It has been more than two decades since urban communities were first created. The practice has played a vital role in satisfying people's everyday needs, conciliating social friction during reform, upholding good social conduct and safeguarding ongoing reform. It has also been helpful in building a harmonious socialist society. In general, the urban community management system has witnessed two phases of development since the founding of the PRC.

1. Neighborhood Management under the Planned Economic System

(1) Evolution of residents' committees under the planned economic system

After 1949, the CPC quickly established the unit-based social management system in cities where an overwhelming majority of urban residents became members of individual units. The unemployed, those eligible for social relief, entitled groups, housewives and all others belonging to no unit were brought under the management of sub-district and residents' committees. This being the case, the unit-based system and sub-district committee system supplemented each other to constitute the general framework of the urban social management system. By virtue of the unit-based system and the sub-district committee system, the government brought about the classified management of urban residents. Both systems were accountable to the government, the former being in charge of the management of people belonging to units and the latter responsible for managing those related to no unit.

The sub-district committee system is a grassroots organizational form of social management with sub-district offices and residents' committees as vehicles. Sub-district offices and residents' committees took shape at the beginning of our founding when administration of the government in urban grassroots communities was dominated by sub-district governments. That is to say, sub-district offices or governments were then the primary-level urban regimes or basic government agencies established by the state as it took over cities based on those 'offices of takeover committees'. In 1953, Peng Zhen, in his capacity as mayor of Beijing, presented to the central government the *Report on the Funding and Organization of Urban Sub-district Offices and Residents' Committees* in which he suggested that urban residents' committees should be established. He said that residents' committees were self-governed mass organizations rather than polities or the 'feet' of political organizations. Though urban residents' committees were not governmental in nature, he continued, it was necessary to establish them as representative offices of cities or districts so that they could help alleviate the burden of district governments and police substations in assembling unorganized residents who belonged to no factory, enterprise, institution or educational establishment.[35] The report won central government approval and in 1954 the Standing Committee of the NPC formulated and issued the *Organic Rules Governing Urban Sub-district Offices* together with the *Organic Rules Governing Urban Residents' Committees* that defined the nature, position, function, responsibility, organizational structure, relationship with relevant departments and units, and financial resources of sub-district offices and residents' committees. From then on, the sub-district committee system in China's urban grassroots management was established.

Of particular importance was the germination of 'household committees', which were tantamount to residents' committees under the unit-based system. Since units had to be responsible for managing the livelihood of their staff and workers, most established their own living quarters that integrated the functions of dormitories and service facilities. Generally, all these living quarters had their household committees directly under the leadership of the units. As in the case of residents' committees, household committees used to be the lowest-ranked and self-governed social management organizations in cities prior to the implementation of reform. The difference was that they were merely management organizations within units since they did not acknowledge the leadership of, nor had any association with, the 'local' governments of the sub-districts where they operated.

---

[35] Wang Zhenyao and Bai Yihua. *Neighborhood Work and Construction of Residents' Committees* [M]. Beijing: China Social Sciences Press, 1996, pages 179-181

(2) Changes in the role of residents' committees under the planned economic system

A. Changes in the role of sub-district offices

After the initial establishment of sub-district offices, their jurisdiction was not large, the people involved were not many and their tasks were relatively simple. In the *Organic Rules Governing Urban Sub-district Offices* issued in 1954, it was stipulated that sub-district offices had three tasks: handling neighborhood affairs designated by the governments of cities or districts, guiding the work of residents' committees, and reporting residents' opinions and demands to local governments. In actual fact, sub-district offices only played supplementary roles in social management because those they served were merely limited to the aged, the sick and the disabled beyond the unit-based system and their duties were restricted to areas such as household policies, relief, the urban environment and sanitation.

Since the 1990s, urban sub-district offices have strengthened their functions and gradually assumed a role bordering on government. Currently, sub-district offices undertake at least 10 tasks: first, development of the 'sub-district economy'; second, management of cities in areas such as urban environment and sanitation, municipal facilities and urban landscaping; third, civil affairs concerning public welfare undertakings, consolation and relief, and marriage registration; fourth, community services such as services for the elderly and disabled, mental health services, services of benefit and convenience to the public, and folk customs reform services; fifth, management of the population involving family planning, labor and employment, and the transient population; sixth, governance of social security such as law popularization, civil mediation, security and safeguarding, and maintenance of social order; seventh, socialist cultural and ethical construction, including the development of culture, education, scientific activities, sports and healthcare in communities; eighth, public administration and undertakings assigned by district governments; ninth, supervision of the work of community committees and reporting to the local government residents' opinions and demands; and tenth, reinforcement of party building in communities.

B. Changes in the role of residents' committees

The *Organic Rules Governing Urban Residents' Committees* promulgated in 1954 made palpable the role of sub-district committees: offering public welfare services related to residents; reporting to local governments or their representative offices the opinions and demands of residents; motivating residents to respond to government policies and abide by the law; overseeing public security; and mediating in disputes between residents. In the late 1980s, the role of sub-district committees increased slightly. In line with the *Organic Law of Urban Residents' Committees of the PRC* issued in 1989, sub-district committees were obliged to assume the following duties: first, propagating the constitution, laws, regulations and state policies, safeguarding the legitimate rights and interests of residents, guiding residents to perform their obligations according to law and protect public property, and carrying out activities of socialist cultural and ethical construction; second, conducting public affairs and welfare for residents in their residential areas; third, mediating disputes between residents; fourth, assisting in the maintenance of social security; fifth, assisting people's governments or their representative agencies in performing their duties in public health, family planning, consolation and relief, adolescent education and other affairs that have a bearing on the interests of residents; and sixth, reporting to people's governments or their representative agencies the opinions and demands of residents and bringing forward their own advice.

(3) Features of sub-district committees under the planned economic system

The sub-district committee system that took shape in the era of the planned economy and which featured a 'strong state and weak society' was supplementary to the unit-based system in function and therefore had many properties *sui generis*, of which the most peculiar were its being controlled solely by the government and its being auxiliary or subsidiary in organizing and managing urban residents.[36]

A. Absolute control by the government

As in the case of the unit-based system created in the planned economy, the state exercised rigid and even absolute control over sub-district offices and residents' committees, particularly in terms of finance and personnel appointment and displacement, to the extent that relevant laws and regulations only existed nominally. The *Organic Rules Governing Urban Sub-district Offices*, promulgated in 1954, stipulated that directors, deputy directors and secretaries of sub-district offices should be assigned exclusively by municipal districts or people's committees of cities without sub-districts.

---

[36] Lei Jieqiong. *Urban Grassroots Community Organizations in Transition – Studies on the Grassroots Community Organizations and Development of Communities in Beijing* [M]. Beijing: Peking University Press, 2001, pages 35, 197-198

In fact, the key leadership of sub-district offices set up after 1958 were all designated by higher authorities. It was stipulated in the *Organic Rules Governing Urban Residents' Committees* that each residents' team should elect one committee member, and candidates for directors and deputy directors should be mutually nominated among committee members. In reality, however, all committee members, including directors and deputy directors, were appointed by the street committee or by internal appointment. As with finance, it was specified in the *Organic Rules Governing Urban Sub-district Offices* that all office expenses and staff salaries of sub-district offices should be appropriated by people's committees of provinces or municipalities. It was also stipulated that all incidental office expenses and extra subsistence allowances of residents' committees should be appropriated by people's committees of provinces or municipalities. In this way, through their absolute control of personnel appointment and financial power, superior governments exercised control over sub-district offices and residents' committees.

B. Auxiliary in functions

After the mid 1950s, the Chinese government primarily exercised control over and coordination of society by means of the unit-based system. Sub-district offices and residents' committees came into being because some residents who belonged to no unit had to be brought under management, which is why we now believe that sub-district offices and residents' committees were auxiliaries of the unit-based system. The system was characterized by a number of peculiar features. First, the primary targets of sub-district offices and residents' committees in management were the aged, the sick, the disabled, housewives and others who belonged to no unit. All these vulnerable groups were among the non-labor forces in cities and largely marginalized in government management. Second, residents' committees initially were only responsible for maintaining social order and security, doing cleaning, mediating disputes and conflicts, and other work. Since their activities were non-productive and non-political, sub-district offices and residents' committees were naturally auxiliary and secondary compared with those units that assumed significant roles in politics, the economy, culture, education, mobilization and management.

Since sub-district offices and residents' committees were auxiliary in nature, they constituted urban grassroots organizations that played crucial roles in maintaining urban order, mobilizing residents, providing services of benefit and convenience to the public, developing the community economy, and increasing employment in the context of a planned economy. With the deepening of reform and the transformation of society, this primary-level management system became more outdated and there were calls for pressing reform and innovation when its defects increasingly came to light.

2. Community Management under the Market Economic System

(1) Evolution of community management system

The construction of urban communities was the natural continuation of social services in a new context. Since the late 1980s when community services thrived in China, calls grew for enhancing the construction and development of communities. With the advance of the economy and society, and deepening of reform, the integration of government administration with community management and the combination of government functions with enterprise management prevailing in the planned economy could no longer keep pace with the times. The organizational structure of society was transformed in China and the functions of social organization structurally changed in a big way with the breakdown of the unit-based system when 'unit men' became 'social men' or 'community men' and functions such as social services and management were splitting off enterprises and government sectors. As the one and only type of management mechanism, the sub-district organization system could no longer satisfy the demand of multi-functional communities. In this context, reform of the urban community management system was becoming imperative.

At the beginning of the 1990s, China brought forward the idea of community construction and started pilot projects in a number of cities. In December 2000, the General Office of the CPC Central Committee and the General Office of the State Council jointly forwarded the *Ministry of Civil Affairs' Opinions on Promoting the Nationwide Construction of Urban Communities* in which community was defined as a social group of people who inhabited a certain region. It further noted that the scope of urban communities generally referred to the administrative regions whose scale had been readjusted with the reform of the community system. The promulgation of the document marked the overall start of urban community construction across the country.

After 2002, the construction of urban communities in China entered a phase of constant improvement and deepening. It was stated in the *Report of the 17th CPC National Congress* and the *Decision on a Number of Major Issues on Building a Harmonious Socialist Society* passed at the Sixth Plenary

Session of the 16th Central Committee of the CPC that urban communities should be built into social groups that are harmonious and well civilized, with ordered management and perfect service. It was an idea that highlighted the overall goals of community construction with Chinese characteristics. In the given context, ordered management refers to perfect organization, specific responsibility and rational mechanism in management. In communities, party organizations must play leading roles, the democratic consultation system and all systems of democracy must be sound and standardized, and residents should be the masters of their own destiny in management of grassroots society, economy, politics, culture and other public affairs so that a dynamic self-governing system of residents under the leadership of the party would be created. The security system must be improved, the network of mass prevention and governance and the mechanism for addressing social conflicts must be complete, government administration and self-management of communities should be connected effectively, and government administration according to law and self-management of communities by law must be integrated so that communities are well ordered and residents enjoy their life and work to the full. 'Perfect service' means that communities should be equipped with public facilities and varied services so that they could offer their residents diversified and personalized services. 'Harmonious and civilized' means that residents should have faith in science and be committed to learning, that cultural and ideological progress should be promoted, that learning families and organizations should be widely established, that residents should willingly abide by laws and disciplines, that families and neighbors should be well-mannered and respectful, that scientific, healthy and civilized life style should be universally formed, and that residents should foster the consciousness of social morality and awareness of environmental protection.

(2) Basic framework of China's urban community management system

According to the *Ministry of Civil Affairs' Opinions on Promoting the Nationwide Construction of Urban Communities* jointly forwarded by the General Office of the CPC Central Committee and the General Office of the State Council, governments at all levels should take on leadership, civil affairs sectors should play leading roles, departments should cooperate and coordinate, residents' committees should sponsor and organize, social forces should supply support and the public should participate intensively so that the integrated framework for community construction would be brought into being. Based on these practices, the current community management of China has taken shape.

A. Leadership of party committees and governments

To strengthen their leadership in community construction, government departments of all provinces and cities and their representative agencies (sub-district offices) have established coordinating organizations of community construction to be responsible for the routine work of communities within their administrative regions.

B. Regulation by civil affairs departments

The Primary Political Authority and the Management Division subordinated to the Ministry of Civil Affairs, the competent functional department in charge of construction of communities, are jointly responsible for community construction, their primary obligations being conducting investigations, formulating regulations, directing and coordinating, and inspecting and supervising.

C. Relevant departments as competent entities

Community management is a systematic project that entails cooperation and coordination of all related sectors. Take the practices of district-level governments. Generally, steering committees in charge of community construction are set up at the levels of district committees and governments. The top leaders of district committees, governments, people's congresses and political consultative conferences assume the posts of directors and deputy directors, while the key leaders from more than 20 sectors including organization and publicity departments of district committees, bureaus of civil affairs, finance and urban administration of district governments constitute the members of steering committees. In this light, they are both collective decision-making agencies and collective authorization institutions. Community construction offices subordinated to steering committees are based in civil affairs bureaus that supervise the implementation of obligations of all government departments and coordinate relations between competent departments on behalf of steering committees. This system design allows the interactive mechanism governing each department to take form (see Figure 6-1).

D. Neighborhood communities as organizers

Residents' committees, within the authorization of the national constitution and laws as well the decrees and regulations of the government and in compliance with the rights and obligations stipulated in the *Organic Law of Urban Residents' Committees of the PRC*, exercise authority in the discussion, coordination, service, supervision and management of community affairs, and conduct democratic self-governance of communities under the leadership of community party organizations and with the guidance of district governments, sub-district offices and various competent sectors.

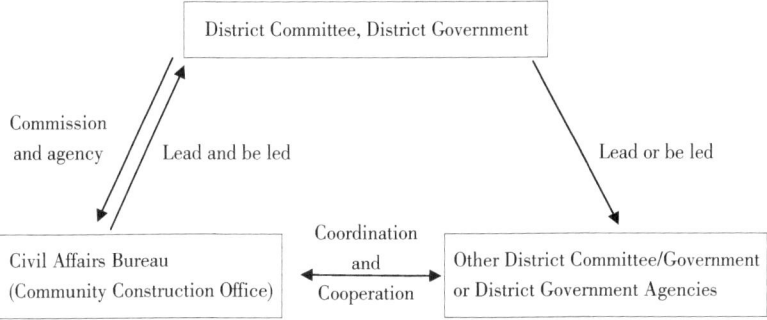

Figure 6-1 Interaction between government sectors in community management
Source: Ding Maozhan. *Reform of China's Urban Community Management System* [M]. Beijing: China Economic Publishing House, 2009, page 52

E. Extensive participation of social forces

The construction of communities is a systematic project that calls for the engagement of government and non-government organizations as well as the wide participation of community residents and social forces. As is pointed out in the *Ministry of Civil Affairs' Opinions on Promoting the Nationwide Construction of Urban Communities*, construction of communities entails maximum resource sharing, joint development and extensive participation of organs, groups, the army, business organizations, government institutions and other forces within communities.

(3) Progress towards a community management system – orientation of reform

With the advance of society and the economy in China, the demands on improving the community management system are getting more pressing. Since 1991, when the Ministry of Civil Affairs proposed the idea of community construction, China's community management system has undergone continuous progress and improvement. Their functions having been constantly expanded, urban communities that have already developed into places of congregation for diversified social groups, confluences of various interests, footholds of multi-faceted social organizations and pivots of the party's government of society have been playing increasingly significant roles in satisfying public demand, integrating interests, mediating social conflicts and maintaining social stability. However, with the progressive drive of reform and opening up and sustained growth of the socialist market economy, social management is becoming more challenging, with profound changes in China's economic system, social structure, interests pattern and people's ideology. As a consequence, it is imperative that urban management abilities should be strengthened, social stability should be safeguarded and social harmony should be promoted through reforming the community management system.

The ultimate goal of innovation in the community management system is to establish a robust and reliable foundation for building a harmonious socialist society based on the existing system by bringing into being a modern governance structure. In this structure, community units act in close coordination and community residents participate extensively with community party branches as the core, social self-governing organizations as the base, community service stations as the pillar, and community social organizations as the supplement by means of integrating social resources and attracting extensive participation of social forces. In this way, a new pattern of community governance adapted to the socialist market economy will be constructed to further bring into being a community governance system and operating mechanism in which the regulation mechanisms of government and society interconnect, the functions of government administration and social self-governance are complementary, and the forces of government management and social synergy interact.[37]

II. Urban Community Services in China

Community services in China reflect Chinese characteristics since they have been established by integrating welfare and social services based on the country's realities of social security. At the start, community services took shape and developed with the advocacy of the government and civil affairs departments. At the 16th National Congress of the CPC, the principle of 'expanding community services in order to make life easier for the people' was written into the party's political report for the first time in its history. In April 2006, the State Council promulgated the *Opinions on Strengthening and Improving Community Services* in which it was pointed out that a community system should be set up that adapts to the socialist market economy and covers all community residents with diversified service principals, perfect

---

[37] Ding Maozhan. *Reform of China's Urban Community Management System* [M]. Beijing: China Economic Publishing House, 2009, page 52, Chart 2-1

service functions and relatively high service quality and management level so as to raise people's living standards and quality of life. It was the first official document issued by the State Council in the development of China's community services that energetically gave full expression to the state's concerns with the public's right of a basic livelihood.

1. Properties of Community Services in China

Community services in China aim to deliver public, welfare and convenient services to all community members, including community residents and units within communities. The aim is to satisfy the mounting physical and cultural needs of community members under the leadership of the party and government by relying on the support and participation of non-governmental organizations, related government sectors and their representative agencies as well as self-governing mass organizations, by mobilizing community forces and by pooling community resources. In this light, community services in China include free or inexpensive public and welfare services, and involve inexpensive and paid services that are convenient and beneficial to community residents.

In the era of China's planned economy, community services used to feature a top-down supply model operated by the government alone. With the transition of society and the economy, community services began to assume some new properties in their cooperation and integration with the government, society and market. First, service principals tended to be diversified. While the government was the main provider of community services, a number of non-governmental organizations, self-governing mass groups and private enterprises had begun to participate in the manufacture and supply of community service products. Second, the objects or targets of service were varied, encompassing residents, special populations, vulnerable groups and units within communities. Third, the properties of services were varied, including public and welfare services such as social care, relief and assistance, as well as services convenient and beneficial to the public. Fourth, the types of service multiplied with the co-existence of government administrative services, social mutual services and market-based services.

2. Community Services in Today's China

Driven by government administration, China's community services have been progressing since the mid 1980s and playing pivotal roles in promoting economic development, sustaining social stability and uplifting the living standards and quality of the public.

(1) Preliminary progress in construction of community facilities

By the end of 2010, there were 84,689 urban communities countrywide, which had established 30,021 comprehensive community service stations, 3,515 neighborhood community service centers and 693,000 public convenience service outlets, along with numerous community health centers or stations, community cultural centers and other specialized community facilities.

(2) Constant expansion of community services

Labor and employment, social security, subsistence relief, cultural entertainment and other public affairs have become accessible to communities. The enrollment and registration system of community service volunteers has been exercised extensively and voluntary mutual services have boomed. The construction of supermarkets, vegetable markets, breakfast stands and other commodity networks has been highlighted. Household services, estate management, elderly care and pre-schooling, food distribution, repair services, waste recycling and other projects have made life easier for residents and helped improve their quality of life.

(3) Sustained increase in community service staff

Members of residents' committees have been elected according to law, full-time community staff have been publicly recruited from society and a multitude of qualified urban and rural residents have joined in community services. Moreover, a growing number of residents have become volunteers active in community services and played important roles in community construction.

(4) Continuous promotion of community service models

Relying on community service centers and stations, many places have put into practice one-stop services and in the meantime promoted the informatization of communities so as to satisfy the varied needs of residents as efficiently as possible by means of modern information technology. Some places have invigorated their own community services and the service capacities of social organizations through government purchase of services, the establishment of funded projects, supply of subsidies for projects and participation of social organizations, enterprises and public institutions as well as residents in community management and service.

(5) Initial formation of community service system environment

The state has issued laws and regulations on securing the rights and interests of the aged, the under-aged and the handicapped and has promulgated policies on community health, social assistance, labor and employment, culture and education, community service facilities and others. Policies and measures have been adopted for promoting community services across the country, laws and regulations for community services have been steadily perfected, party committees and governments of all levels have been lending weight to community services, and community residents have been increasingly identifying themselves with community services.

Despite the fact that considerable progress has been made in the construction of China's community service system, several hurdles have yet to be cleared. With the speeding up of economic development and urbanization in China, communities have already turned into places where various social groups and conflicts congregate. Problems confronting current urban community services in China include a scarcity of service facilities and an inadequate number of places for services in some communities. The contents of community services need to be enriched and disparities between supply and demand are acute. Talented personnel engaged in community services need to be strengthened and the quality and structure need to be improved. The community service system and mechanism in need of unified planning should be optimized. Insufficient investment, lack of coordination and redundant construction are pronounced. The integration of resources is inadequate and the mechanism of social participation is to be perfected. In this light, to address the problems with the system and mechanism is central to the development of community services in China.

3. Prospects for Urban Community Services: Transform Government Functions and Develop NGOs

(1) Transformation of government functions as the prerequisite for developing urban community services

The historical development and administrative characteristics combine to determine the crucial role of the government in community services and the practice of government-led community services has constituted the inevitable form of community services in China during the process of development. That is to say, the Chinese government has been playing a significant part in promoting the initiation and growth of community services and it would be impossible for China to have achieved such progress in community services within a short time without the drive and intervention of the government. However, with the transition of China's economy and society, problems experienced by the government in community administration, such as overreaching itself and being absent, are constantly exposed, so much so that they have already harmed the sound development of community services. The limits of government capacity have given rise to the inefficient operation of community agencies and failed to meet the diversified and specific demands of residents in a timely manner. The government has now been confronted with various conflicts in community services and stunned to realize that it has to press for the transformation of its functions so that its role and capacity will be well coordinated. With the transformation of functions, the 'unlimited government' will be translated into a 'limited government' so that its limited functions in community services will be given full play. In the meantime, diversified community service principals should be fostered to assume the functions yielded by the government.

(2) NGOs as structured vehicles in transforming government functions

The Chinese government has been working to give full play to NGOs and turn them into the leading suppliers of community services. In April 2006, the State Council promulgated the *Opinions on Strengthening and Improving Community Services* (hereafter referred to as the *Opinions*) in which it claimed that NGOs should be fostered in the community services sector, particularly those providing services for the aged, minors and the handicapped along with those applying themselves to the public good, charity and mass-oriented cultural and sports activities. Conditions should be created for NGOs to start operations and, where conditions permit, the right to use some community service facilities could transfer to NGOs, places and office equipment required for operation should be supplied and qualified staff should be recruited for them through competition so as to strengthen coordination between service organizations. Volunteer service in communities should be standardized, an incentive mechanism for volunteers should be established and participation of mass organizations composed of people from all walks of life in communities as volunteers should be bolstered. The *Opinions* further noted that NGOs should be supported and given full play in undertaking community services. Residents should be encouraged to set up various charitable organizations, mass-oriented cultural and sports groups and popular science societies as well as organizations that provide services for the aged, the handicapped and the poor. The promulgation of the *Opinions* demonstrated that the government was lending increasing weight to the role and position of NGOs in community services in its advocacy and was shoring up NGOs as the main supplier of services.

(3) Fostering, development, administration and supervision equally underscored as the basic principles for managing community NGOs

Fostering and development means encouraging and bolstering the growth of NGOs in a way that is conducive to social progress. By reinforcing administration and supervision, illegal NGOs and those violating the law will be investigated and cracked down on, according to the law. Only the integration of fostering and development with administration and supervision can promote the healthy growth of NGOs. Take Shanghai as an example. Based on its actual realities, Shanghai worked out a hub-like system for the management of NGOs. The 'hub-like system' is essentially a management vehicle set up between government sectors and NGOs, acting as a service center for community NGOs that is responsible for organizing services for, and management of, NGOs within communities in aspects of party building, operations and security. These service centers for NGOs have been established at the levels of sub-districts (towns) and districts and perform the following duties in managing NGOs registered according to law within the jurisdictions: establishing archives for party members employed by NGOs within the jurisdictions; carrying out party building and effectuating overall coverage of all community NGOs in terms of party construction; integrating the human resources of NGOs within the jurisdictions and reinforcing dynamic management; underwriting insurance for endowment, health and unemployment for NGO staff; conducting proactive evaluations and surveys on newly-established NGOs within the jurisdictions and writing opinions and suggestions after assessment; organizing professional training and consulting services associated with NGOs, providing them with information and holding seminars and symposiums; offering various paid intermediary services; and forewarning illegal NGOs and assisting relevant departments in investigation. The staff required in service centers should be employed by means of open recruitment in combination with internal assignment based on the principle that full-time personnel should outnumber part-timers. The funds of service centers are guaranteed with financial subsidies by means of government-purchased services along with other adequate subsidies from party membership dues. Budgets must be reasonable and expenditures should conform to regulations. Offices of service centers are provided largely by sub-district committees. By means of hub-like management, effective administration of and full services for NGOs have been achieved, at least in communities when the responsibilities of fostering, development, management and supervision have been carried out well. In summary, the hub-like system of management has provided an operating platform of socialized administration for promoting the transformation of government functions, improving social management modes, reinforcing the ruling foundation of the party and strengthening the self-development of NGOs.

Special Column 6-1 'Service circles within a quarter' established in Chaoyang district in Beijing aimed at promoting the well-being and satisfaction of citizens

By constructing 'service circles within a quarter' as a support, Chaoyang district in Beijing succeeded in improving community services, satisfying public demand, mobilizing social participation and strengthening the building of harmonious communities.

By the beginning of 2011, Chaoyang had set up 119 'service circles within a quarter'. During the construction of 'service circles', government functional departments, community service stations, volunteer organizations, units based in communities, enterprises and individuals all played full roles. The district, in its effort to do well in community public services, services for public good and virtual services, lent powerful support to the building of 'service circles within a quarter'.

First, a catalog of community public services has been formulated to buttress such services. The catalog functions as a 'basic menu' that gives community residents free access to all basic public services delivered by the government. At present, item 97 of the catalog has already been exercised at the grassroots level.

Second, volunteer services have been well promoted to support services for the public good. The city's first 'public savings center of volunteers' has been established in the district with sub-centers set up in sub-district offices and varied service stations put up in communities and business buildings. Relying on the website of the 'public savings center of volunteers', the district has integrated resources of different sectors and established a real-name database of volunteers. And by means of deposit or saving of time, spiritual incentive and others, the district, in its call to 'work as volunteers if you have spare time and asking volunteers for help when you have trouble', has set up platforms for exchange of volunteer services and image display.

Third, regional service resources have been integrated to support convenience services in communities. Socialization has constituted the central principle of community services. Insisting on pursuing social benefit with economic efficiency as the means, the district has brought together the resources of social units based in communities and has tried to constantly enrich the contents of service. The district has been working to intensify the opening of the public service facilities of schools, the army and other social units to residents. Today, 83 schools, colleges or universities have opened their sports facilities to society and more than 160 units have opened their canteens, conference rooms, sports grounds and sports facilities to residents. In this way, problems with public recreational and sports activities have been addressed. In addition, all sub-district committees have been integrating banks, post offices, hospitals and other social units within their jurisdiction and encouraging them to deliver services for residents.

Fourth, information technology has been applied to support community virtual services. The district has been giving full play to modern information technology as it promotes the informatization of community services. It has coordinated all hotline resources of the district government and promoted the systematization of consultation, complaints, community services and monitoring of public livelihood by further improving the functions of hotlines, community service networks, SMS and MMS. In addition, all sub-district committees and communities have set up their own 'virtual communities' so that they may satisfy the individual demands of residents.

Fifth, social organizations have been fostered to promote professional services. Social organizations within communities are important coordinators of community services. Coordinating committees of social construction have been set up in all the 23 sub-districts, and coordinating committees of public affairs have been established in all communities. The third-party coordinating agencies of social construction have been put up as platforms for people from all sectors of society to express their views and participate in social construction. The district has also established social work offices together with professional agencies and institutions of higher education and participated in community services by means of service purchase and project operation.

III. Self-governance of Urban Communities

The long-term goal of community construction is to achieve self-governance of communities by residents. As is stated in the *Ministry of Civil Affairs' Opinions on Promoting the Nationwide Construction of Urban Communities* jointly forwarded by the General Office of the CPC Central Committee and the General Office of the State Council in November 2000, self-governance of communities by residents shall be exercised under the leadership of the party and the government. Put another way, self-governance shall be practiced at the levels of self-governance, self-service, self-election and self-supervision, and its aim is to realize democratic election, decision-making, supervision and management.

1. History

Self-governance of communities by residents in China means neither federalist autonomy nor collective self-rule in an absolute sense; nor does it border on absolute local autonomy. Self-governance organizations in China's communities are subject organizations in communities, namely community committees of residents whose members are generated through democratic elections and are responsible for the management of daily affairs. Community committees of residents are in nature mass self-governing organizations through which community residents exercise self-governance, self-education, self-service and self-supervision under the leadership of the party.

In line with the Constitution promulgated in 1954, the state worked out and passed the *Organic Rules Governing Urban Residents' Committees* in which it was stipulated by law for the first time that residents' committees were "mass self-governing organizations of residents" and thereafter construction of residents' committees was launched across the country. After 1958, particularly during the Cultural Revolution when several grassroots self-governing organizations of the masses were demolished, including residents' committees; democracy at the primary level got bogged down in the crisis. It was not until after the reform and opening up was under way that the development of democracy at the grassroots level was restored. On January 19, 1980 when the state reissued the *Organic Rules Governing Urban Residents' Committees* passed in 1954, the urban grassroots self-governing system started to resume development. Based on the *Organic Rules Governing Urban Residents' Committees*, the *Organic Law of Urban Residents' Committees of the PRC* was passed by the Standing Committee of the NPC. Thus far, the primary-level self-governing system in cities was brought under the protection of the law.

2. Basic Framework

(1) Leadership of the party as the core

At present, party organizations have been established in all communities, including community party committees and general party branches, under which are party branches. The establishment of party branches in residents' committees marks the most striking difference between democracy at the grassroots level in China and that in western countries. China's choice of its system is justifiable in that it guarantees the exercise of self-management, self-education and self-service of residents without deviating from the overall direction of socialist development. As far as residents' committees are concerned, the establishment of party branches in residential quarters facilitates implementation of the party's mass line so that the committees will better exercise residents' self-governance under the leadership of the party.

(2) Construction of residents' committees as the pivot

It is stipulated in the *Organic Law of Urban Residents' Committees* that urban residents' committees are self-governing organizations of the masses through which community residents practice self-governance, self-education and self-service. The framework of the community residents' self-governing system comprises: community party branches – the center of leadership; residents' representative conferences of communities – the core of procedure for decision-making; community committees of residents – both executives and decision-makers during the adjournment of residents' representative conferences of communities. As the leading organizational carrier of residents' self-governance, it does not transform the grassroots and self-governing nature of residents' committees, nor does it change the dominant role of residents' committees in residents' self-governance.

Institutionally, the framework of residents' self-governance of communities gives prominence to the role of residents' committees as key organizational carriers. As far as institutional construction is concerned, the conference system of residents' representative assemblies, residents' meetings and others are established and perfected along with the setting up of financial and auditing systems. Take Shaojiu Community in Beijing's Donghuamen sub-district, for example. Today, more than 70 community systems of every description have been established here. In the meantime, the community has set up residents' groups, volunteer teams and other organizations with the assistance of the residents' committee. As regards operational mechanism, the election system of residents' committees has been improved. For instance, in the general election of residents' committees conducted in Beijing in 2003, almost every sub-district had a pilot direct election by means of which residents' committees were elected at residents' representative conferences and subject to their supervision. During the pilot election reform exercised by Jiudaowan Residents' Committee, Dongcheng district, Beijing, the will of the residents and the tenet of self-governance was highly regarded in choice of election model, nomination of preliminary candidates, determination of official candidates and germination of the residents' committee. Moreover, the conventional performance evaluation system has been transformed and some indicators for performance appraisal with residents' committees as the subjects of evaluation have been canceled. Instead, residents have become the subjects of appraisal and their satisfaction has been taken as the yardstick for evaluating the actual performance of residents' committees.

(3) Serving all residents as the focus

Functionally, the systematic framework of residents' self-governance has generated new features in promoting the traditional role of residents' committees:

- **A. Macroscopic planning**

    In their efforts to satisfy residents' demands, most communities across the country have worked out their unified planning of development and set down their short-, medium- and long-term goals and tasks of development.

- **B. Decision-making**

    Residents' meetings and representative conferences are held to discuss and work through major issues and matters of pubic interest in communities.

- **C. Organization and management**

    Since residents' committees offer services for all, they have to organize and call on residents to conduct self-management, self-education and self-service as it is impossible for them to address the many thorny issues on their own.

- **D. Coordination and communication**

    Residents' committees are devoted to both create a harmonious and peaceful community environment and coordinate between resident representatives and the government or property management companies for the interests of all.

E. **Supervision of communities**

Social workers are invited by residents' committees to report on their performance at a given time and suggestions will be made based on the exercise of their work.

In general, the role of residents' committees is to wholeheartedly comply with the will of urban residents and provide services for all community residents.

3. Case Study: Innovative Self-governance of Weifang Sub-district, Pudong New District

After continuous exploration for more than a decade, Weifang Sub-district in Pudong New District succeeded in finding a new way to implement residents' democratic self-governance that featured 'four selfs', as follows:

(1) Self-election of residents' committees

As early as 1999, Daoyuanzhu Residents' Committee in Weifang Sub-district achieved success in a pilot 'direct election'. The practice was further assumed by 14 residents' committees in 2000 and 'mass-election' was adopted in all Weifang's 27 residents' committees as of 2006. By means of 'mass-election', those enthusiastic in community services and strong in social mobility and practice came to the forefront and their participation was manifested in the rights of grassroots residents to self-manage their own communities. This showed that residents' committees had become more trustworthy self-governing organizations that work to represent, safeguard and promote the interests of the masses.

(2) Self-decision on major issues

Residents' committees as channels for delivering public opinions and places where conflicts of interest are mediated and resolved are closely related to many major issues in residents' public life. With the coordination of committees, the self-governance of residents is achieved through consultation. Take Yiju Community in Weifang Sub-district, for example. The primary-level government once invested heavily in its own initiative to improve the living environment of the community. The endeavor, however, failed to be recognized by all residents. Families with private cars called for a widening of roads in communities, while people without private cars were set against it. Confronted with this dilemma, the sub-district committee eventually managed to win the approval of all by soliciting opinions from all sides before working out proposals and inviting every resident to participate in the making of the final decision.

(3) Self-organization of mass organizations

Weifang Sub-district now has 200 cultural organizations self-organized by residents that hold regular activities covering sports and fitness, culture and art, education and reading, and popularization of science. These various events have attracted extensive resident participation and helped promote the cultural progress of communities and residents' skills.

(4) Self-management of communities

Residents of communities are actively engaged in volunteering and participation in the self-governance of communities. The attachment of residents to their communities has increased and many residents are racing to enter into community services. By 2011, Weifang Sub-district Committee had established 27 volunteer service stations, 37 model units engaged in volunteering, around 100 volunteer teams and more than 10,000 volunteers.

Chapter 7

Protection of Urban Historical and Cultural Heritage in China

I. Protection of Urban Historical and Cultural Heritage in China: Past and Present

Broadly, cultural heritage is either tangible or intangible. Intangible cultural heritage includes drama, music, folklore and festival ceremonies, while tangible cultural heritage contains both movable cultural relics such as antiques, calligraphy and paintings and immovable cultural antiquities such as ancient ruins, architecture and cave temples. Immovable cultural relics, such as ancient sites, towns, neighborhoods or villages and famous cities of historical and cultural value are accounted for in the *Law of the PRC on Protection of Cultural Relics*, and are equivalent to 'cultural heritage' that has been internationally recognized, are actually referred to in a broad sense. For those engaged in urban planning in China, ancient sites, towns, neighborhoods or villages and famous cities of historical and cultural value are frequently identified with historical and cultural heritage and, barring those intangible and movable relics, they could be recognized as cultural heritage in a narrow sense. In this chapter, both 'cultural relic' and 'cultural heritage' are used in the narrow sense.

1. Before Reform and Opening Up

China boasts a wealth of cultural heritage as it has 5,000 years of history and is home to 56 nationalities. Due to historical reasons, however, protection of China's cultural heritage started much later than in Europe. From the late 19th century to the early 20th century when imperialist powers invaded China, some scholars and missionaries from Europe and the US arrived, many of them with the aim of plundering antiquities and wealth. Protection of cultural relics in China began in the 1920s when archeological research began to thrive. In 1922, Peking University established its institute of archeology and archeological academy, the first institution for academic research of heritage protection and preservation in China's history. In June 1930, the then government promulgated the *Law on the Protection of Antiques* and soon after issued the *Detailed Regulations Regarding the Law on the Protection of Antiques*. In 1932, the Central Committee of Heritage Preservation was established. Due to political unrest and warfare, however, many cultural relics were neglected across the country at a time when laws and regulations were only in nominal existence.

After 1949, faced with the massive destruction and considerable losses of antiques during wartime, the Chinese government issued a package of decrees, set up central and local administrations, established archeological institutions and worked out various measures for the protection of cultural relics. By the mid-1960s, the system of protection for China's cultural relics took preliminarily shape. During this period, the government focused primarily on the protection and preservation of individual ancient architectural structures including buildings, historical sites as well as scenic spots and places of interest. In March 1961, the State Council published the *Provisional Regulations on the Protection and Control of Cultural Relics*. In the meantime, it brought out the first 180 key historical sites under state protection and implemented a protective system in which cultural relics and historic sites were designated as 'sites of cultural and historical value'.

The Cultural Revolution that started in 1966 wreaked havoc upon the laws and regulations of the country and it was only natural that protection of cultural relics would suffer huge losses.

2. After Reform and Opening Up

Historical preservation and urban planning administration was revived after 1978. In 1982, the State Council published a second group of key historical sites under state protection when, in February of that year, the first 24 famous cities of historical and cultural value under state protection were made known. The protective system of historical cities in China was now under way. In November 1982, the *Law on the Protection of Cultural Relics* was promulgated. In January 1984, the State Council issued the *Ordinances on Urban Planning*, in which it was stipulated that protection of cultural relics and historic sites should be heeded, while national styles and local features should be well preserved and protected in urban planning. In 1986, the State Council listed another 38 famous cities of historical and cultural value under state protection, having further stipulated that ancient architectural complexes and towns, neighborhoods or villages of historical and cultural value should be protected and that all provinces could bring out their own local famous cities of historical and cultural value. The protection of cultural heritage in China expanded from places where historic buildings and architectural complexes were located to certain urban areas and beyond. The system for protecting famous cities of historical and cultural value was therefore established and the graded protective system of China's historical and cultural relics took shape (see Special Column 7-1).

Special Column 7-1 Graded protection of historical and cultural relics in China

Historical and cultural relics under protection in China, unlike those in other countries, break down into three types: sites protected for their historical and cultural value; towns, neighborhoods or villages of historical and cultural value; and famous cities of historical and cultural value. With regard to sites protected for their historical and cultural value, the principle of preserving the historical contours of the original places applies. In protecting towns, neighborhoods or villages of historical and cultural value, the overall style and exterior appearance of architectural structures should be kept intact, although internal alterations or modifications are permitted in the latter case. As for famous cities of historical and cultural value, construction is allowed in places where no tangible or intangible historical and cultural relics are found provided that the overall layout and features of old towns or cities are preserved during construction. The graded or differentiated protection of historical and cultural relics congruent with the prevailing situation in China helps address any conflicts between preservation and construction.

With the booming growth of the urban economy and a marked rise in real estate after 1990, many towns, neighborhoods or villages of historical and cultural value were demolished, the protection and preservation of historic environment having been confronted with new predicaments. In response, the Ministry of Construction and the State Administration of Cultural Heritage jointly set up the Committee of Experts on the Protection of Chinese Famous Cities of Historical and Cultural Value in March 1994 so as to strengthen supervision and technical consultation in protecting famous cities and assist local governments to better protect and manage famous cities of historical and cultural value. Moreover, with the aim of improving and promoting the protection of historical and cultural heritage according to law, the State Administration of Cultural Heritage promulgated the revised *Law on the Protection of Cultural Relics* in 2002, the Ministry of Construction issued the *Code of Conservation Planning for Historic Cities* in 2005, and the State Council published the *Regulations on the Protection of Famous Historical and Cultural Cities, Towns and Villages* in 2008.

II. Protection of Urban Cultural Relics and Historical Sites in China

1. Methods and Principles

Cultural relics and historical sites include sites of ancient cultures, ancient tombs, ancient architectural structures, cave temples, stone carvings, murals that are of historical, artistic or scientific value, and important modern and contemporary historic sites, material objects and buildings that are related to major historical events, revolutionary movements or famous personalities and that are highly memorable or are of great significance for education or for the preservation of historical data. As is stipulated in the *Law on the Protection of Cultural Relics*, the Chinese government implements protection of various important historical sites and other immovable cultural relics recognized by the state as sites of historical and cultural value in terms of their historical, artistic or scientific value. Today, there are 60,000 county-level famous historical sites, 7,000 provincial key cultural sites and 1,268 sites of historical and cultural value under state protection across the country.

The *Law on the Protection of Cultural Relics*, as the legal basis for the national protection of cultural relics and historical sites, has set down the principle for historic preservation. It gives priority to the protection of cultural relics, attaching primary importance to their rescue, and making rational use of and tightening control over them, the purpose of it being to preserve and carry on the overall historical value and message. All protective measures exercised shall be in compliance with the principle that the original state of historical and cultural relics shall remain unchanged.

2. Laws and Regulations on Protection of Urban Architectural Heritage

According to the *Law on the Protection of Cultural Relics*, ancient architectural structures are among the key cultural heritage to be protected. As is stipulated in Article 17, no construction of additional projects or operations such as blasting, drilling or digging may be conducted within the area of protection for a historical and cultural site. However, where under special circumstances it is necessary to conduct construction of additional projects or operations such as blasting, drilling and digging within the area of protection for such a site, its safety shall be guaranteed, and the matter shall be subject to approval by the people's government that formerly verified and announced the site and which, before giving approval, shall ask consent of the administrative department for cultural relics under the people's government at the next higher level; and where construction of additional projects or operations such as blasting, drilling and digging are to be conducted within the area of protection for a major historical and cultural site protected at the national level, the matter shall be subject to approval by the people's government of the relevant province, autonomous region or municipality directly under the central government, which, before giving approval, shall ask consent of the administrative department for cultural relics under the State Council.

On the basis of the actual need for the protection of cultural relics and with the approval of the people's government of the relevant province, autonomous region or municipality directly under the central government, a certain area for control of construction may be drawn up around a site protected for its historical and cultural value. No construction of a project in an area for control of construction may deform the historical features of the site protected for its historical and cultural value. No facilities that pollute the sites protected for their historical and cultural value or their environment may be put up within the area of protection for these sites or the area for control of construction, and no activities that may adversely affect the safety and environment of these sites may be conducted. Where there are already facilities that pollute the sites and their environment, they shall be brought under control within a specified time limit. When choosing a place for a construction project, the construction unit shall try its best to avoid the site of immovable cultural relics and where it is impossible to do so under special circumstances, it shall do everything it can to protect the original site protected for its historical and cultural value. Where it is impossible to protect the original site or the site needs to be moved to another place or dismantled, the matter shall be reported to the people's government of the relevant province, autonomous region or municipality directly under the central government for approval; where a site protected for its historical and cultural value at the provincial level needs to be moved to another place or dismantled, consent of the administrative department for cultural relics under the State Council must be obtained prior to approval. No major historical and cultural sites under state protection may be dismantled; where such a site needs to be relocated to another place, the matter shall be reported by the people's government of the relevant province, autonomous region or municipality directly under the central government to the State Council for approval.

On top of that, specific provisions have been made for the rights and obligations in protecting historical architectural structures in Article 21 of the *Law on the Protection of Cultural Relics*: users of state-owned immovable cultural relics shall be responsible for their repair and maintenance; and the owners of the immovable cultural relics not owned by the state shall be responsible for their repair and maintenance. Where the immovable cultural relics not owned by the state are in danger of damage and the owner cannot afford their repair, the local people's government shall offer the owner assistance; and where the owner can afford their repair but refuses to perform their obligation to do so as required by law, the people's government at or above county level may make emergency repairs and the expense incurred shall be borne by the owner. In the meantime, in repairing, maintaining and removing immovable cultural relics, the principle of keeping cultural relics in their original state shall be adhered to. Moreover, in compliance with the stipulation in Article 22, where immovable cultural relics are totally damaged, the ruins shall be protected and the damaged relics may not be rebuilt on the original site.

3. Keeping Intact the Original Forms of Historical Construction

In 1982, the principle of keeping cultural relics in their original state was written into the *Law on the Protection of Cultural Relics*. It made clear that this principle shall be adhered to in repairing, maintaining and removing immovable cultural relics. In line with the principle, 'four preservations' shall be adhered to in repairing and maintaining ancient buildings: preservation of the original state, preservation of architectural structure, preservation of construction material and preservation of technology. Not unnaturally, the principle helps secure the authenticity and integrity of historical constructions. As ancient architecture is evidence of history, the preservation of intact historical space and cultural memory helps people trace back to the remote past and place themselves in the genuine context of bygone days.

The principle of keeping cultural relics in their original state requires a series of measures to vouch for the preservation of historical architectural structures. First of all, it is crucial to respect history. We must think highly of the positive contributions of all historical ages to the construction of ancient architectural structures and conduct careful identification and remove traces of repair by later generations in an attempt to restore them to the state of the known historical time. Second, importance should be attached to the preservation of originals. Reinforcement of original structures should be focused on preservation, while eliminating hidden perils in repairing original structures. Third, historical features must be preserved. Authenticity should be retained as much as possible and traces of modern intervention should be reduced. Fourth, evaluation and research should be strengthened. Value estimates and assessment of the current condition of structures should be conducted and substantial measures for preservation and repairs should be worked out to prolong the life of historical buildings. Fifth, technical innovation should be promoted. New techniques and materials should be applied to reinforce the structures of ancient architecture based on scientific research and experiments. Sixth, intangible cultural heritage must be protected. In repairing and maintaining ancient buildings, traditional craftsmanship, techniques and materials should be used so that technical historical skills will be preserved and passed on.

Special Column 7-2 Protection of the Potala Palace in Lhasa, Tibet

The Potala Palace in Lhasa is among the largest and best-preserved palace-style architectural complexes in the world. In 2002, the palace witnessed the launch of a second round of a comprehensive preservation and maintenance project.

In line with the principle of following the original design, maintenance staff first carefully surveyed and studied the texture and all components of the palace before starting repair work. Since the overall structure of the palace could be divided into different parts that were inconsistent with one another in terms of construction time, function and technique, it was necessary for them to have each part individually surveyed, mapped and analyzed before working out a plan for maintenance and preservation. They also studied the construction materials and traditional craftsmanship peculiar to Tibet. While integrating traditional techniques with modern technology, they applied new techniques and materials to reinforce the palace so as to make up for the weaknesses of traditional materials and techniques and promote the inheritance, perfection and development of preservation techniques of cultural relics (see Figure 7-1).

Figure 7-1 Preservation and maintenance of the Potala Palace completed (F Bbu Zahi, Xinhua News Agency)

III. Protection of Historical and Cultural Street Districts in Chinese Cities

1. Definition and Principles

As is stipulated in the *Law on the Protection of Cultural Relics* promulgated in 1982, towns, neighborhoods or villages with an unusual wealth of cultural relics of important historical value shall be verified and announced as famous places of historical and cultural value. In the *Regulations on the Protection of Famous Historical and Cultural Cities, Towns and Villages* jointly drawn up by the Ministry of Construction and the State Administration of Cultural Heritage (draft for examination and approval), historical urban districts – towns, neighborhoods or villages of historical and cultural value – are defined as places of considerable scale with relatively rich historical remains, cultural relics, and modern and contemporary historical sites and buildings that authentically and perfectly reflect the traditional style and local features of a certain historical period. The definition has highlighted 'traditional style' and 'considerable scale' and thus marked the distinction between urban districts of historical and cultural value and sites of historical and cultural significance in terms of scale.

Three principles have been worked out for protecting urban districts of historical and cultural value. The first is protecting authentic historical remains, which is tantamount to protecting cultural relics and historical sites. The second is protecting the overall exterior style and features, which is distinct from the protection of cultural relics and historical sites. It means that internal restructuring and renovation are permitted and that the focuses of protection also include architectural environment and others that are separate from the relics and the sites proper. The third is preserving and giving play to the original usability. In other words, what is preserved should also include the social and cultural activities and functions the relics and sites assume so that they will stay active and their lives will be prolonged.

2. Outline of Planning

First, the scope and dimension of a protection area for the control of construction around a site protected for its historical and cultural value shall be determined. A historical urban district shall simultaneously satisfy the requirements of three established criteria for urban districts of historical and cultural value in terms of scope of protection: historical authenticity, true to life and integrity of style and features. Historical authenticity means that a certain quantity and proportion of authentic physical or substantial entities such as historical architectural structures that bear historical information should markedly dominate the ambience or atmosphere of a historical urban district. The quantitative criterion for historical authenticity is largely based on the time when the structures within the historical urban district were established. In general, the proportion or floor area of ancient architectural structures within China's historical urban districts that manifest the time of traditional buildings of distinct styles and features should reach around 50%. By true to life, it means that historical urban districts are not only places that used to be residences, but places that are and will be playing their roles as natural and organic components of social life. There are two criteria for judging true to life, the first being the measurable retention rates of former residents and the second the qualitative retention rates of original lifestyle. That is to say, an urban district of historical and cultural value should be a place where traditional culture and lifestyle are strikingly distinctive and have been best preserved in the city or district. Put another way, the retention rates of original traditional lifestyle should be the highest in the district. Today, the population retention rates in China's historical urban districts will have to be as high as around 60% so that the style and structure of social life within the districts will be kept intact and, meanwhile, the original residents retained will be satisfied in terms of current national residential standard and modern standard of living.

Integrity of style and features as a criterion can also be defined. First, the style and features within reach of a historical urban district should be essentially consistent with the visible environment, relatively integrated and preservable. Second, an urban district of historical and cultural value should be adequate in scale. In determining the scale, two aspects should be taken into account: the scale of the historical urban district should not be much too large in delimitation because it is the place where construction of a project is banned and the historical features are to be renovated and preserved; in the meantime, the area delimited should not be much too small considering that there should be relatively integrated features and a comparatively complete structural system of social life within the district. In this light, the proportion of historical features and architectural structures satisfying the criteria should stand at about 50%, and not less than 30%. Poorly located buildings and those with inferior features should account for about 20% of the total and no more than 30%. In addition, an urban district of historical and cultural value should be limited in size, the suggested area for the key zone to be preserved being 15-30 hectares with a total area of around 30-55 hectares.

Second, measures for preserving and renovating historical structures shall be worked out. For identified sites protected for their historical and cultural value or those to be identified as such according to planning, measures specific to sites protected for their historical and cultural value shall be exercised. For historical buildings whose original styles and features are better protected, the appearance of the originals shall be preserved though additional facilities that are much needed in modern life may be included in the renovation. For those suffering serious internal damage, the internal structure could be replaced while preserving the historical appearance. New buildings that are sympathetic to the historical environment could be kept unchanged. For new buildings such as huge modern constructions that clash with the historical styles within an urban district of historical and cultural value, renovation should be conducted, for example by restructuring façades, removing some floors or complete dismantlement.

Third, requirements for preserving and renovating environmental factors or elements of historical urban districts shall be formulated, including maintenance of roads and revetments and protection of mature trees.

Fourth, municipal facilities shall be renovated and reconstructed within historical urban districts to help address problems with the likes of rainwater and sewage systems, power supply, telecommunications and firefighting.

To wrest tighter control over vandalism of urban districts of historical and cultural value, the Ministry of Construction published the *Measures for the Administration of Urban Purple Lines* in November 2003 in which the purple lines were delimited for historical urban districts within national famous cities of historical and cultural value, historical urban districts listed by the people's governments of provinces as well as historical constructions recognized by people's governments above county level. It was stipulated in the Measures that the purple lines should include key districts under protection and peripheral zones where any construction is controlled. Architectural structures protected within the purple lines should not be dismantled; newly constructed or reshaped buildings should not be built in the traditional layout and style of a historical urban district; and gardens and greenbelts, rivers and lakes, roads, and mature and precious trees reserved according to planning should not be vandalized.

3. Successful Cases in Recent Years

Since the system for protecting historical street districts was established in China, considerable progress has been made in the preservation and renovation of historical street districts. Here are some successful cases.

(1) South Avenue in Pingyao

Located in Pingyao County, Jinzhong City, Shanxi Province is the Old Town of Pingyao, one of the famous state-level towns of historical and cultural value that enjoys a history of more than 2,700 years. In 1977, when renovation started with South Avenue that runs through the center of town, all overhead electrical cables and telecommunications lines were relocated underground

Figure 7-2 View of South Avenue in Pingyao after renovation (Fan Minda, Xinhua News Agency)

and all asphalt roads were restored to stone paving along which residents were encouraged to run stores and hold exhibitions of folk art. After renovation, the original historical style and features of the district were well preserved, and the economy thrived with the development of tourism (see Figure 7-2).

(2) Lijiang

The Old Town of Lijiang in Lijiang City, Yunnan Province, is among the second group of famous towns of historical and cultural value approved by the state. Making use of funds appropriated by the state for preserving and protecting historical urban districts, the government has reconstructed the drainage and lighting in the district and restored its original historical style and features, which in turn has helped promote the preservation of the old town and its economic growth (see Figure 7-3). Today, the Old Town of Lijiang and the Old Town of Pingyao, both well-known tourist attractions in China, have succeeded in their application for world cultural heritage status.

Figure 7-3 View of the Old Town of Lijiang (Lin Yiguang, Xinhua News Agency)

(3) The Old Street of Tunxi in Huangshan City

The Old Street of Tunxi in Tunxi District, Huangshan City, Anhui Province has been identified by the Ministry of Construction as a pilot urban historical district under state protection. During the renovation, the government has funded infrastructure improvements while residents have paid for finishing their own storefronts. After renovation, it has become a must-see for those visiting Mount Huangshan, and tourism around the street has developed rapidly (see Figure 7-4).

Figure 7-4 The Old Street of Tunxi in Huangshan City (Wanglei, Xinhua News Agency)

(4) The Old Street of Wuzhen in Tongxiang City

Situated in Tongxiang City, Zhejiang Province, Wuzhen is a time-honored town whose historical style and features have been well preserved. Since 1999, when a specialized institution was set up in Tongxiang, policies have been drawn up[38] for the renovation of the environment and architectural structures in the district in a planned way, resulting in the successful

---
[38] Tongxiang City has established a specialized institution for the protection and development of Wuzhen, namely the Management Committee of Protection and Tourism Development of Wuzhen Town. The policies it has formulated include the *Management of Housing Relocation for Protection and Tourism Development of Wuzhen Town*, the *Management Ordinances for the Protection and Development of Wuzhen Town*, and the *Opinions on Speeding up Protection and Tourism Development of Wuzhen Town*

restoration of the original historical style and features. During the renovation, old materials were used to replace or repair old houses, streets and bridges so as to reproduce the original features of the old street. All overhead electrical cables and telecommunications lines have been relocated underground and flush toilets have been installed along the street. Today, the Old Street of Wuzhen is enjoying rapid development (see Figure 7-5).

Figure 7-5 The Old Street of Wuzhen in Tongxiang City (Tanjing, Xinhua News Agency)

IV. Protection of Historical Cities in China
1. Definition and Criteria for Selection
(1) Definition of historical cities

According to the stipulation in Article 8, Chapter 2 of the *Law on the Protection of Cultural Relics* published in 1982, cities with an unusual wealth of cultural relics of important historical value or high revolutionary memorial significance shall be verified and announced by the State Council as famous cities of historical and cultural value.[39] A concept native to China, 'famous cities of historical and cultural value' is slightly distinct from the way things operate in foreign countries. In effect, the concept does not mean preservation of a city at large. Besides, the contents and scale of protection are determined by means of urban planning.[40]

---

[39] *The Law of the PRC on the Protection of Cultural Relics*, Article 8
[40] Wang Jinghui. *The Role of Urban Planning in Cultural Heritage Protection: Interaction between Urban Planning and Protection of Cultural Relics* [J]. *China Cultural Heritage Scientific Research*, 2006, (1)

(2) Criteria for selection

Selection of famous cities of historical and cultural value in China is primarily conducted in line with three criteria. First, the city chosen must have a long history with a wealth of well-preserved cultural relics and historical sites, as well as significant historical, scientific and artistic value. Second, the current structure and style of the city should retain historical features with a known number of districts representing the city's traditional properties. Third, the cultural relics and historical sites should be largely distributed in downtown or suburban areas, and protection and fair use of this historical and cultural heritage will positively affect the city's make-up, layout and formulation of construction policies.

2. Features of Historical Cities in China

Famous cities of historical and cultural value in China have the following two features:

(1) Large in number

There are now 101 famous cities of historical and cultural value under state protection in China promulgated by the State Council: 24 in 1982, 38 in 1986, 37 in 1994 and two in 2001. In this regard, China boasts the largest number of famous cities of historical and cultural value in the world. For instance, there are only four famous cities under state protection in the UK. Unlike China, however, the UK focuses on preservation and protection of conservation areas, cultural relics and historical sites. Statistically, there are as many as 500,000 nationally listed architectural structures[41] and 8,000 conservation areas in England alone.

(2) Complex in type

Based on the distinct factors that constitute history, nature, human geography, urban material elements and urban functional structures, the 101 famous cities of historical and cultural value under state protection can be broken down into seven types: cities as ancient capitals characterized by a wealth of historical remains and features; cities with traditional styles and features that have retained intact architectural complexes of one or more historical eras; cities of scenic attraction in which the natural environment plays a decisive role and the dynamic integration between architectural structures and natural environment constitutes their pronounced distinctness; cities of regional and

---

[41] The practice of cultural properties being nationally listed is widely adopted for the preservation of history in western countries

ethnic features located in ethnic places and manifesting unique characteristics, ethnic customs, regional cultures and peculiarities of their own due to the effect of geographical diversity, cultural environment and historical change; cities significant in modern and near modern history that are distinguished by a certain historical event or by their historical constructions or architectural complexes of a certain period; cities with special functions, of which at least one used to be extremely significant in history and constitutes their present distinctness; cities that have a wealth of cultural relics and widely dispersed historical sites to constitute their traditional features.

3. Principles and Contents of Protection

(1) Principles of protection

The formulation of principles for protecting famous cities of historical and cultural value aims to protect cultural heritage in cities and promote the growth of the urban economy and society in order to constantly improve the living and working environments. Cities are organic entities in which tens of thousands of people live and work. For the development of the economy and facilities, and for the betterment of people's living standards and the realization of modernized cities, the wealth of historical and cultural resources should be exploited to the full by protecting famous cities of historical and cultural value so that they will be given full play in boosting the development of the urban economy, society and culture.

(2) Contents of protection

Three aspects have to be taken into account in protecting China's famous cities of historical and cultural value: the first is the protection of historical and cultural sites as well as regions of historic significance, of which the protection areas can be delimited; the second is the protection and preservation of historical arrangements and features of ancient cities by means of working out catalogues of management measures and standards of control in urban planning; and the third is inheritance and the carrying forward of fine historical and cultural traditions, which entails the efforts of competent departments and sectors of urban planning as well as the common concerns of the public.

> **Special Column 7-3 Overall protection of the Old Town of Suzhou**
>
> It is remarkable, at an international level, that the site of the Old Town of Suzhou in Suzhou City, Jiangsu Province has never changed since it was founded more than 2,500 years ago. Covering an area of 14.2

square kilometers, the Old Town of Suzhou was the first in China where global or overall protection was practiced. The historical layout and features of the town have been well preserved over the years. Compared to the 1980s, the skyline of this time-honored town has remained unchanged. In 2003, when the master planning of the city was once again modified, 29 historical sites were delimited and the *Provisional Regulations on the Compulsory Contents in Urban Planning* were formulated, in which measures for protecting the overall style and features of the old town were stipulated with regard to the height, color, form and size of constructions. The government took the national lead in its application of an urban purple line by means of which it worked to incorporate the protection of the old town and cultural relics into the compulsory contents of its master urban planning. On October 26, 2012, another initiative for protecting the old town was brought out by the government when the Suzhou Conservation Area of the National Famous City of Historical and Cultural Value was officially established. The government's persistent efforts to protect and preserve the Old Town of Suzhou provide a cherished example for the overall protection of historical towns or cities across the country.

In protecting famous cities of historical and cultural value, global views and comprehensive protective measures combine to constitute the tenet and attributes of the effort and in the meantime help create conditions for protecting cultural relics and historical sites while promoting the development of urban construction. The measures to be taken include determining social and economic development strategies suited to the protection of historical cities, working out a rational urban layout and orientation of development in protecting old towns and developing new districts, and improving the functions of old towns in protecting their spatial patterns and visual corridors between key cultural landscapes so that the cultural relics and historical sites will be highlighted. In non-historic or recently developed regions within a famous city of historical and cultural value, limitations of taste and appropriateness also apply to new construction projects in consideration of the city's overall pattern. For a famous city with profound historical and cultural heritage, historical traditions should be highly regarded and promoted.

Special Column 7-4 Hangzhou: the win-win development strategy in constructing new urban districts while protecting the old town

One of China's seven ancient capitals and well-known for its West

Lake and other places of interest, Hangzhou was among the first group of famous cities of historical and cultural value to be put under state protection. Since the reform and opening up, it has been identifying the establishment of a famous city of historical and cultural value as well as protection of cultural heritage with primary productive forces. It has coordinated the twin goals of protecting the famous old town and constructing new districts in its urbanization and found the optimal balance point. Based on its principle of 'constructing new districts while protecting the old town', the city government has been focusing on protecting its old urban district because it is clear that the West Lake, the layout of the old district shaped like a waist drum and the outline known as 'a city enshrouded in cloudy hills on three sides' will be well protected in its effort to keep intact the old town.

As it builds new districts, the government is focused on construction, industry and relocating the population from the old town to new districts. With the construction of Qianjiang New City, Hangzhou has left behind the 'age of the West Lake' and entered the 'era of the Qiantang River' in its burgeoning urban development. Over the past decade or more, the overall layout and scale of the new city along the Qiantang River have taken shape, during which time a huge number of people and industries have aggregated in the new urban area. As the pressures and burdens on the old town moderated, the government has scored win-win achievements in its effort to protect the old town and promote the economic development along and across the Qiantang River.[42]

---

[42] Wang Guoping. *Cities: Where to Go?* [M]. Beijing: People's Publishing House, 2010

Chapter Follow-up Questions and References

Chapter 1

Questions

1. How does China's urbanization relate to that of the world?
2. How does the historical development of China's urbanization differ from that in your country? And why?
3. What are the Chinese government's policies with regard to the country's urbanization?

Bibliography

1. Chu Tianjiao & Tan Wenzhu. *Urban Planning and Management in Rapid Urbanization* [M]. Beijing: People's Publishing House, 2012
2. Zhou Ganzhi. *A Probe into Urbanization with Chinese Characteristics* [J]. Urban Planning International, 2009, (S1)
3. Li Jingwen. *Major Trends of Development in China's Urbanization: Rise of Urban Clusters and Their Demand for Investment* [J]. Innovation, 2008, (3)
4. Gao Xincai, Zhou Yi & Xu Jing. *On the History of China's Urbanization* [J]. Academic Exchanges, 2010, (1)

Chapter 2

Questions

1. What should we do to address the relationships between the 'rigidity' and 'flexibility' in urban-rural planning within the context of rapid urbanization?
2. How should we bring into effect urban-rural planning so that diversified capital would be brought in to urban construction?

3. What effect have different political and economic systems generated in the administrative system of urban-rural planning and its operating system?

Bibliography

1. Chu Tianjiao & Tan Wenzhu. *Urban Planning and Management in Rapid Urbanization* [M]. Beijing: People's Publishing House, 2012
2. Dong Jianhong. *History of Cities in China* [M]. Beijing: China Architecture & Building Press, 2004
3. E. Howard, *Garden Cities of Tomorrow* [M]. Translated by Jin Jingyuan. Beijing: the Commercial Press, 2002
4. Geng Yuxiu. *Management of Urban Planning* [M]. Shanghai: Shanghai Science and Technical Literature Press, 1997
5. Li Dehua. *Principles of Urban Planning (third version)* [M]. Beijing: China Architecture & Building Press, 2001

Chapter 3

Questions

1. What effects does economic globalization have on the spatial layout of urban industrial structure?
2. How does the government-led construction of new urban districts attract diversified capital?
3. How can we do a good job of addressing the relationship between developing new urban districts and promoting the functions of old urban districts?

Bibliography

1. Chu Tianjiao. *Evolutionary Trend of the Structure of Manufacturing Industry in the Yangtze River Delta* [J]. World Regional Studies, 2010, (3)
2. Contemporary Shanghai Research Institute. *Research on Urban Development in Contemporary Shanghai* [M]. Shanghai: Shanghai People's Publishing House, 2008
3. Wang Fengyu & Zhu Xiaojuan. *China Development Zones Development Review and Strategic Thinking* [J]. Yunnan Geographic Environment Research, 2006, (4)
4. Yu Hongjun & Ning Yuemin. *Outline of Urban Geography* [M]. Hefei: Anhui Science and Technology Press, 1983

5. Zheng Guo. *Growth of Development Zones and Reconstruction of Urban Space in China: Implications and History* [J]. Modern Urban Research, 2011, (5)

Chapter 4

Questions

1. What phases of construction of urban infrastructure has China gone through? And what are their main features?
2. How should the financial problems in China's urban infrastructure be best addressed? And what innovative initiatives should be adopted in reforming its systems and mechanisms?
3. What enlightenment and inspiration can we draw from the construction of urban infrastructure in China?

Bibliography

1. Liu Xuexin. *Risks in Market-based Reform of China's Infrastructural Industry* [M]. Beijing: Science Press, 2009
2. Jiang Shijie. *Investment in Infrastructure and Progress of Urbanization* [M]. Beijing: China Construction Industry Press, 2010
3. Gao Jian & Wang Xiongjian. *Leverage of Investment Strategies in China's Urban Infrastructure on Economic Growth* [M]. Beijing: Peking University Press, 2009

Chapter 5

Questions

1. What are your thoughts on China's property rights system?
2. What means or measures do you think are applicable to the regulation of land market supply and demand? How should regulatory policies for land market supply and demand be best coordinated with fiscal and financial policies? And in what way could a satisfactory regulation effect be achieved?
3. How can the utilization efficiency of urban land be enhanced?

Bibliography

1. Bi Baode. *Studies on China's Land Market* [M]. Beijing: China Renmin University Press, 1994
2. Chu Tianjiao. *Patterns of Land Negotiation and Their Standardization* [J]. Shanghai Economic Forum, 2002, (4)

3. He Fang. *Development and Innovation of the Land System with Chinese Characteristics* [J]. Shanghai Land Resources, 2012, (3)

Chapter 6

Questions

1. What effects could different economic systems have on urban community management?
2. What more efforts do you think China should make in its transition from community management mode to community governance mode?
3. What should the party do to promote the sound development of residents' self-governance and strengthen its leadership?

Bibliography

1. Chen Xian, et al. *Community Economy and Services* [M]. Shanghai: Shanghai University Press, 2001
2. Cheng Yushen. *Studies on the Development of China's Urban Communities* [M]. Shanghai: East China Normal University Press, 2002
3. Lin Shangli, et al. *Community Organizations and Construction of Residents' Committees* [M]. Shanghai: Shanghai University Press, 2001
4. Lu Hanlong. *Organizational Construction of Community Services* [J]. Quarterly Journal of the Shanghai Academy of Social Sciences, 2002, (2)
5. Ma Xiheng & Liu Zhongqi. *Governance of Urban Communities: with Reference to Construction of Shanghai into an International Metropolis* [M]. Shanghai: Xuelin Publishing House, 2011
6. Peng Bo. *Changes in Contemporary China's Urban Communities* [M]. Beijing: China Social Publishing House, 2007

Chapter 7

Questions

1. How have the ideas and concepts of protecting urban cultural heritage in China evolved?
2. What are the means by which urban cultural heritage in China have been well protected?
3. What new practices has China promulgated to protect its urban cultural heritage?

Bibliography

1. Ruan Yisan, Wang Jinghui & Wanglin. *Protection of Historical Cities: Theory and Planning* [M]. Shanghai: Tongji University Press, 1998
2. Shan Jixiang. *Retaining the 'Root' and 'Soul' of Urban Culture: Exploration and Practice of China's Cultural Heritage Protection* [M]. Beijing: Science Press, 2010
3. Wang Lin & Wang Jun. *Formulation of Planning for Protecting Urban Historical Districts* [J]. Urban Planning, 1998, (3)
4. Wang Jinghui. *Protection of Historical Sites: Theory and Applications* [J]. Urban Planning, 1998, (3)
5. Robert Riddell. *Sustainable Urban Planning* [M]. London: Blackwell Publishing Ltd, 2004
6. Stephen M. Wheeler. *Planning for Sustainability* [M]. London: Routledge, 2004